THE TRAVELS OF GAIUS

A Masonic Tale of Allusions

BOB W. LINGERFELT

Dedicated to the Nolan

CONTENTS

ACKNOWLEDGMENTS

I would like to extend my gratitude to MWB Thomas Hauder for his review and input on early drafts of this book. Tom is a fellow member of the Grand Lodge of Nebraska's Education Committee and an educator who can be depended upon to deliver entertaining and informative presentations on a wide variety of Masonic topics. Without his feedback and encouragement, this book might have remained nothing more than an idea.

I would also like to mention two other members of our Education Committee, WB Dennis Byrdl and WB Jonathan Paz, with whom I have had many fascinating discussions about Freemasonry's history and development. These three brothers, and still others, are a constant source of inspiration. It is my great hope that I might capture and convey even a fraction of that inspiration to others.

FOREWORD

> The splendid story had begun sometime in the early seventeenth century, one night in Lucerne or London. A secret benevolent society...was born; its mission: to invent a country.
>
> Excerpt from *Tlön, Uqbar, Orbis Tertius*, by Jorge Luis Borges

What follows is a story, a fictional tale, intended to familiarize newly initiated Freemasons with certain fundamental Masonic principles. I am using this unorthodox educational approach because it allows me to create a world within which I can create memorable connections between some Masonic tenets and practices that are otherwise only tenuously related, if at all.

The story is a hero's journey of the type prevalent in ancient myths and modern novels and movies. In it, an adventurous young man, escorted by his guide, moves from a land of darkness into a magical world of light. There, he faces many dangers in his pursuit of an elusive master who might help him find something of great value. Our hero's name is Gaius (pronounced Guy-us), a name so ubiquitous in ancient Rome that it evolved into a generic term for *any* man. Our hero thus represents any man, though, in particular, any man who chooses to become a Freemason.

Nothing in this story should be taken too seriously. In fact, the story is silly at times. But as I pointed out in another of my books, *Solomon's Memory Palace*, silly and outlandish things are better remembered than things that are predictable and mundane. Since the objective of this story is to help a new Mason learn and associate certain fundamental elements of our craft, it necessarily contains a fair amount of brain-stimulating absurdity and exaggeration. I admit to taking tremendous creative liberties here and there to establish plot continuity and to make the story, and its underlying lessons, fun and accessible to the novice Masonic student. I have done so with an expectation that the reader will, at some later date, conduct more serious investigations into the topics which interest him.

Because the rituals and specific teachings of Freemasonry differ from region to region around the world, there are bound to be ideas, characters, and utterances within the story that will make no sense to some readers, even if they are perfectly understood by others. Nevertheless, the foundational concepts of our fraternity are universal, and I have tried to focus on those things we have in common, versus our differences, whenever possible.

There are no Masonic secrets here – by which I mean, no secrets that Masons are sworn to conceal and protect. However, members of our craft have, for centuries, demonstrated a remarkable zeal for seeking out hidden and lost things. For that reason, I have concealed a few *things* here and there within the story. Perhaps they will be found quickly. Perhaps, not at all. Time will tell.

If you find this story helpful, or at least entertaining, I would very much appreciate a positive review. There are a great many books about Freemasonry, but relatively few new books are written *by* Freemasons *for* Freemasons. A kind review of this book by a brother will help distinguish it from these other varieties.

Thank you – and now, on with our story!

Bob Lingerfelt, P.M.

Education Committee of the Grand Lodge of Nebraska, A.F.&A.M.

Bellevue Lodge #325

Saints John Lodge of Education #331

Tabula Rasa Lodge #332

Scottish Rite, Omaha Valley

S.R.I.C.F.

CHAPTER 1

THE CALL

There was once a thing of great value that was lost. The nature of the thing was a secret, but in all ages, there were men who were born with an innate sense of its existence. These men spent their lives traversing the world seeking clues about the thing's history, properties, and, above all, where it might be found.

Because these men had a common cause, they gained permission from their king to form an Order of knights, so that they might share their findings with one another, and safeguard the clues they collected for future generations. They established gathering places around the world where they could rest safely during their long journeys among like-minded men.

The tabards and armor of these knights – whether plate, chain, leather, or cloth - was peculiar in that it was as white as newly fallen snow. This was so that anyone who might encounter a knight would know that he was a peaceful man dedicated to the pursuit of knowledge, not war. This immaculate armor stood in contrast to the dented and bloodied armor worn by the land's many bands of roving warrior knights who, displaced by battle, and having no means of sustaining themselves, often plundered homes and farms, bringing chaos and ruin to entire villages. In this way, the white armor of the knights, unstained by blood and unspotted by the world, served as a knight's badge and as an emblem of innocence.

It was rumored that the knights of this Order collected many great and wonderful tales during their travels in foreign lands and that they learned many strange arts and sciences.

Now, there was a young man named Gaius (named after Julius Gaius Caesar, or so he was told), who heard the call of the secret thing and decided he would join the Order. The decision did not come easy, since many of his friends and family warned him that the pursuit of the secret thing was dangerous, or pointless, or immoral, or subversive, or childish. Yet he was steadfast in his convictions and sought out a friend whom he knew was in the Order to ask how he might join.

This friend, named Amicus, knowing of Gaius's sincerity of purpose and good character, recommended him to the Order. A few days later, three men, named Planchet, Boniface, and Grimaud, approached Gaius to inquire about the nature of his interest. Blanchet and Boniface smelled strongly of food, as if they'd spent the entire day cooking, while Grimaud's hands were stained with ink, as if he had spent the day writing.

The men asked Gaius many questions and, to the villager's relief, seemed satisfied with his responses. They advised Gaius that the thing which he sought was real, and was purportedly somewhere in the East. Gaius asked where in the East he should go, and the best route to take, but the three men told him that such information could only be divulged by the Master of their Order. When Gaius asked where the Master was, the knights told him that if he would go to a certain high hill on a certain date, at noon, he would find a guide who knew the way.

A fortnight passed, and when the time came, Gaius made the trek to the hill described by the men who had questioned him. There he found Planchet and Boniface waiting for him. Each wore, atop their armor, a brilliant white tabard on which was the insignia of the Order. Neither was armed, but each carried a long rod, or pole, that was capped by a strange silver device.

"Greetings, friend," said Planchet. "Are you ready to begin your journey?"

"I am," replied Gaius, glad to see familiar faces. He had been worried that the men of the Order might have second thoughts about accepting him. "But why are we gathering so far from the village, on this high hill?"

"We meet here," answered Boniface, "to escape the eyes of spies and the long ears of eavesdroppers. From here, we can see all around us for a great distance. No one can approach without us seeing them. See for yourself."

Gaius slowly pivoted and surveyed the country around him. In one direction, he saw his distant village, smoke pouring from the chimneys, and several farms, and the roads that ran between them. In another, he saw the great forest in which he often collected wood. In another, he saw the wetlands, teeming with life, and in another, the great plains of tall grass he'd played in as a child. Strangely, while all those places were familiar to him, he could not recall having ever climbed this hill. Yet he saw that Boniface was right – there was no way for anyone to approach without being observed by a person on top.

He nodded and asked, "Where do we go from here?"

"Not *we*," said the man, planting his rod in the ground with so much force that it remained standing when he released it. "*You.*"

Planchet planted his own rod into the ground, only three feet away. The two rods were perfectly vertical and just far enough apart that a broad-shouldered man could pass between them. "This is the start of your journey, friend, not ours."

"But you said you would take me to the Master."

"No," replied Boniface, "we said we'd lead you to a guide. That's different, isn't it?"

"The Master is not in this world," said Planchet. "He is in the Unknown World. Unknown to you, anyway. To find him, you'll need a guide. While we are knights of the Order, we do not carry passes that allow us to travel to all the places you need to go. Your guide will, though. His name is Dux."

"When will he arrive?"

"He is already here," replied Planchet.

Gaius again surveyed the land around them. "I do not see him..."

Boniface laughed. "That's because he's on the other side of the door."

"What door?"

"The door just there," replied Planchet, pointing at the ground between the two rods. You need only knock."

Gaius examined the spot that the man pointed at. "But...there is no door on which to knock."

"There is," Planchet insisted. "You just don't see it."

Gaius wondered if he was the object of a joke. "How should I know there to be a door if I can't see it?"

"Well," replied Planchet, "if you try to walk between those rods, you'll run right into it. That'll tell you, eh?"

He grinned at Boniface, and the two men chuckled.

This exchange made Gaius more certain that the two men were trying to trick him. He crossed his arms and said, "I doubt that will happen since there is nothing between those poles but air." He hedged by adding, "Even if I did encounter resistance of some kind, that wouldn't mean there's an invisible door. An invisible wall would offer resistance, too. A wall is not a door."

"Fair enough," countered Boniface, enjoying the impromptu game, "but if the resistance then moves and allows you to step past it, and after doing so you then find yourself in a different place – I mean, a place unlike this one – then that thing would be a *door* and not a *wall*. Do you agree?"

Gaius thought for a moment. "Yes. That would be a door. In theory."

"Well then," beamed Planchet, his arms splayed. "It's settled. All you have to do is knock on the plane between the rods and see what happens."

Gaius saw he had no choice but to play along, so he moved to a place between and slightly behind the two rods, and readied himself to pantomime knocking on a door. He was certain his hand would pass through the air and that Planchet and Boniface would then shriek with laughter at his gullibility. But he told himself that this was an initiation of sorts, and sometimes initiations included a joke played on the initiate. Not playing along might spoil his chances to join the Order.

Yet when his knuckles crossed the vertical plane, they did, in fact, strike something. Something hard. *Something like a door*. The sensation was quite real. He made two more attempts, encountering the same sensation each time, and though he did not use excessive force, each strike was as loud and distinct as a cannon blast. He imagined the sound could be heard for miles.

"It is real enough," he said, confused by the strange effect. "But it might still be a wall and not a door." It was a silly and petulant statement, and he knew it.

"Just you wait and see," said Boniface. He moved to one side of Gaius while Planchet moved to the other. "Best take a step back, friend. Doors open. You have sounded an alarm, and soon enough you'll get your response."

CHAPTER 2

THE UNKNOWN WORLD

The area between the rods began to shimmer and the ground behind them seemed to bend. It was as if a pane of thick, imperfect glass had been placed between the rods and was now distorting the appearance of everything behind it. This distortion became increasingly pronounced until there was nothing but a kaleidoscope of swirling colors.

To Gaius's astonishment, a man emerged from this twisting, colorful illusion. He was thin and middle-aged, with a short gray beard and long gray hair that rested on his shoulders. He was a few inches taller than Gaius and adorned in immaculate white leather armor. He wore no helmet and carried neither weapon nor shield, but in his right hand, he clutched a tall staff capped with a silver ornamental sun. The man's hazel eyes seemed to glow.

He said, "You are Gaius?"

The younger man, still dazed, took a moment to respond. "I am."

"And you seek to discover the Master, and to join our Order, and to search for that which has been lost?"

"I do."

The stranger nodded. "My name is Dux. I am your guide and will escort you to the Unknown World in which the Master resides, and there, through the several Gates, and a place of terrible Darkness. The journey is perilous, and while I am tasked with keeping you safe, you will not be immune to death. The tests and trials are heavy. Knowing this, do you still wish to proceed?"

Gaius was initially at a loss for words, but, prodded gently by Boniface, he replied, "Yes, sir."

Speaking to Boniface, the guide said, "Is he ready? Has everything been done that must be done?"

"Yes."

The other man looked back at Gaius and seemed to be pondering something. After a moment, he said, "Wait here."

With that, the stranger took a step back and vanished from sight, though the colorful portal remained in place.

Alarmed, Gaius exclaimed, "Where has he gone? Why did he not ask me to accompany him?"

Planchet put a hand on the young man's shoulder. "Patience, friend. It is not his decision to make. He will offer his assessment to the Master of our Order and then, if there are no objections, your guide will return."

Gaius nodded but stood uneasily for several excruciating minutes. He had not anticipated being judged even before he had an opportunity to prove himself. He wondered what was happening on the other side of the invisible door.

Eventually, however, the man named Dux did return, appearing from the same thin air from which he'd vanished.

Looking at Gaius's escorts, he said, "You may bring him to the other side."

It was pitch black on the other side of the invisible door. There was no terrain around the men, no ground, and no sky. Nor was there any sound. It was as if the men stood in the midst of a vast plain of endless darkness.

"Does the darkness frighten you?" asked the guide.

Gaius hesitated for a second, then said, "No, sir."

"Are you sure? You find yourself in a strange land in the custody of a man you do not know, having no idea what might befall you."

"I realize that, sir. But I have faith that God will protect me."

His guide smiled, "Well said. Yet be aware that, as you have rightly placed your faith in God, so has my Order placed faith in you. The wonders and perils of this place are a closely held secret. Regardless of what happens, you must never divulge what you see or experience to any citizen of the Known World. Our assessment is that you are a man of conscience – a man who can be trusted. Is that correct?"

"Yes."

Dux nodded, then looked at the two men standing behind Gaius. "Very well. I will take custody of our friend here. You may go."

Planchet and Boniface pivoted and, in a flash, disappeared.

The guide said to Gaius, "Take hold of my arm. It is very dark here and we don't want you to wander into danger."

The younger man obeyed, and he and his guide began moving slowly forward. Gaius found the experience supremely disorienting. Only his guide's arm prevented him from succumbing to vertigo.

He opened his mouth, prepared to bombard the other man with questions, but before he could do so, his guide whispered, "No questions, my friend. Not yet. For now, be silent."

The initiate nodded – what else could he do? – and the men continued to move slowly forward. Occasionally, and without warning, this guide nudged him in one direction or another, as if there was some invisible obstacle in their path. There were so many of these turns that Gaius gave up all hope of ever finding his way back to the portal without his companion's assistance.

Then came a sudden and violent crack of thunder that caused Gaius to shudder. There had been no precursor – no flash of lightning or distant rumbling. There was no smell of rain in the air. He hoped that his guide might provide an explanation or some calming words, but the man remained silent.

The men continued to walk through the void, and a short time later, there was an even louder crack of thunder. Gaius instinctively ducked, terrified by the auditory assault, but his guide continued to lead him forward.

Then came the third and most terrifying clap of thunder, so loud that it almost forced Gaius to his knees. He stumbled, suddenly disoriented, and only managed to stay upright by clinging to the arm of the man beside him.

Now terrified of what might yet come, the traveler made a silent prayer, asking his deity for protection from the dangers that surrounded him.

A point of light appeared in the darkness ahead.

"Ah," said Dux, "Well done."

Gaius was confused. "What have I done?"

"You have invoked the blessing of deity, have you not?"

Gaius, surprised, answered, "Yes."

"That is what was needed for us to escape this darkness. Without such a blessing, this long march might go on forever."

"Do you mean that, until now, we had no destination? That we were moving through the darkness blindly?"

"Just so," replied his guide. "And, truth be told, I was getting quite tired. I'm not as young as you."

The circle of light grew brighter and larger in diameter. Specks of color appeared, and as the circle grew, these specks stretched into lines, and the lines became planes, and the planes became three-dimensional shapes – cubes, spheres, cones, pyramids, cylinders, and others. These shapes then began to assemble, as if being pieced together by an invisible hand, and the surfaces gained texture.

By the time Gaius and his guide reached the circle, the shapes had become mountains, trees, rivers, and cottages, and the young traveler was surprised to feel a breeze pass over him. It carried with it the fragrant scent of flowers.

"This is a portal," guessed Gaius. "Like the one we used to enter the Unknown World."

"That's right," said Dux. "Are you ready to pass through to the other side?"

"Very ready, sir, for surely there is no place as terrifying as this plain of endless darkness. But what is the land on the other side? Are we returning to the Known World?"

"No. The place you see ahead is the southern realm of the Unknown World – my world, and perhaps, someday, yours. It is the first step in your journey."

The guide placed a hand against Gaius's elbow and urged him forward. "Let's go."

CHAPTER 3
THE REALM OF BEAUTY

His guide at his side, Gaius emerged from the portal and found himself on a cobblestone path in a very foreign land.

The contrast between the dark place he'd just left and the beautiful land in which he now stood was almost too much to bear. All around him were rolling hills blanketed by lush, green grass and flowers of every variety and color. There were people everywhere. Some were sitting or reclining on blankets, sipping wine, and talking quietly to one another. Others, whom Gaius presumed to be writers, scribbled away in small journals. There were also several painters standing in front of canvases set on easels. Somewhere in the distance, a woman was singing. Gaius thought the woman's voice was heavenly.

Amazed and a little terrified, Gaius asked, "Are we in heaven?"

His guide chuckled. "No. We are in the Southern Realm."

"Is it like this everywhere? Is it all so perfect?"

"Perfect? No. This isn't a land of perfection. The South is a land of beauty. Everything here – and every person, as you've surely noticed – is pleasing to the senses. However, the beauty takes different forms in different places. This region is famous for its rolling hills, magnificent flowers, and bubbling creeks, but other parts of the realm are home to snowcapped mountains, blue oceans, sandy beaches, rainforests, waterfalls, vineyards, and so forth."

Dux began walking down the path, Gaius in tow.

As they walked, Gaius said, "The people of this land are very lucky."

"Yes," replied Dux. "The food and wine here are fine, as is the entertainment. This is a land of artists, performers, and musicians. One of the most famous residents is a man by the name of Hiram Abiff, who moved here a few years ago from the Kingdom of Tyre. Have you heard of him?"

"No," admitted Gaius, embarrassed at how little he knew about the world outside his tiny village. "Why is he famous?"

"Oh, he has many skills, but he is best known for his eye for beauty – in particular, architectural beauty. He has an uncanny ability to turn even the drabbest of temples or castles into works of art. He is much sought-after. Kings and queens from around the world constantly offer Hiram great riches if he will only agree to oversee the beautification of their castles and palaces."

"He must be very rich, then."

"Not at all. He refuses most of these offers."

"Why?"

"Because Hiram Abiff believes that beauty is one of God's gifts to mankind, and that He should therefore be acknowledged as its true author. Unfortunately, most of the kings and queens who beg for Hiram's assistance seek praise for themselves, not God. They wish to be seen as the author of the beauty they have paid for and to be praised for it by their citizens. You see, it is not the beautification of the buildings that Hiram objects to, but rather the motives of the vain kings who seek his talents."

Gaius said, "Will I meet him?"

"No. Hiram rarely works in the southern realm because there are too few grand buildings or temples here. Painters are poor carpenters, musicians are poor stonemasons, and there are very few skilled laborers." The guide pointed at the horizon. "Do you see the towers in that distant field?"

Gaius looked and, squinting, nodded. "Yes, but barely." Squinting harder, he frowned. "Are those truly towers? They look more like giant trees bent over by some mighty wind."

Dux chuckled. "An astute observation, but yes, they are towers. Of those you can see, some are ten stories in height. Some that have fallen – and most have fallen – were even taller. What you see is but a fraction of all the towers that have been built over many centuries in the South. There are miles and miles of such ruins further out."

"What a shame," replied Gaius. "They would be a wondrous sight, if only they remained upright. What is the cause of the towers' collapse? Are there no lessons to be learned from one collapse that might be used to prevent future disasters? You said this has gone on for centuries. I cannot understand why that would be so."

"The reason is simple, my friend. The people of the southern realm value form over function. Beauty triumphs over all. If an architect tells them that the design of a building or tower is faulty, that it is too narrow or too tall, or that the soil won't support it, the people here will build it anyway if they feel the design is 'a work of art.' They also tend to build on impulse, and far too quickly, which means they sometimes forget certain elementary features, such as doors."

"Doors?" exclaimed Gaius. "Surely not!"

"Yes. And staircases. Roofs, even. You'd be amazed. Anyway, they prefer tall, slender buildings which can be seen from afar. The more people that can see a building's beauty, the better. At least so long as they remain upright."

"I see. But why not build sturdy buildings, and *then* make them beautiful? Their buildings will continue to collapse if they do not change their ways. The beauty will be fleeting."

"Just so. Which is why Hiram Abiff rarely works in this realm. In fact, he is currently employed by a king named Solomon."

"But you said Hiram rarely accepts commissions from kings. What makes Solomon different? Why would Hiram agree to work for him, but not others?"

"Ah," responded Dux, raising a finger. "King Solomon is erecting his temple to God. In other words, the king is not seeking praise for himself, but instead for the Grand Architect of all things. That makes all the difference to a man like Hiram Abiff. Do you understand?"

"I think so."

"Good. Continue to think, and we shall discuss this later. For now, let's be on our way."

The two continued down the path until they came very near an artist who sat cross-legged on one side of the path, a pad of paper in his lap and a piece of chalk in one hand. He was staring intently at what he'd sketched, as if trying to determine what to do next.

Sensing the travelers' approach, he stood quickly and said, "Greetings, friends! Can you spare a moment to offer me your opinion?"

Dux stopped and gave the man a slight bow. "If you like."

The other man nodded and lifted the sheet of paper that contained his work, presenting it to the travelers. On it was written, in a fanciful script, the word "Freedom," surrounded by a variety of flourishes – roses, vines, cupids, and jewels.

Dux pinched his chin between thumb and forefinger, studying the artist's work, but taking far longer than necessary, at least in

Gaius's estimation. Eventually, he said, "Yes, I see what you're doing here. You've used chalk for a reason, yes?"

The other man's eyes lit up. "Yes! Exactly!"

Gaius shook his head. "I don't understand. What reason?"

His guide pointed at the artist's tunic, which was coated in chalk stains. "Do you not see how easily chalk transfers itself from one surface to another? His hands and clothing are coated with its powdery residue. It takes only the slightest touch to leave a trace behind. It moves so freely that it is almost impossible to work with it without staining your skin and clothing."

Gaius considered this. "So, you mean that 'Freedom' is..."

"Self-referential!" blurted the artist, grinning. "Exactly!"

"Brilliant," offered Dux, though curtly. "A true work of art. You are to be congratulated."

Gaius thought that his guide's expression suggested otherwise, but the artist seemed oblivious to the contradiction.

"Thank, you, sir," the man said gleefully. "I cannot tell you how happy I am that someone understands my craft."

"I am glad you are pleased," said Dux, "and I pray you will continue to follow your passion. But, alas, my friend and I have an appointment, so..."

His words were unnecessary. The artist was already rushing away toward another traveler further down the path.

"That fellow sits next to the path for a reason, I think," said Dux. "He savors the good opinion of others. I think we fell into a trap."

Gaius said, "It wasn't bad, though. His little drawing, I mean."

Dux grimaced. "*Eye of the beholder* and all that. Let's be on our way."

The men continued to walk until the colorful flowers that had been ubiquitous were slowly replaced by a luscious blanket of grass that swayed lazily in the fragrant breeze. Here and there were fruit trees full of ripened fruit. There seemed to be a disproportionate number of plum trees present, and these were of a very strange variety, the round fruit of each dangling at the end of an unusually long, straight stem. In this way, the fruits were like pendulums dangling from wires.

The path twisted gently right. Gaius saw what he took to be an enormous tower in the far distance, the sun floating directly above it. Unlike the other towers he'd observed in the South, this one appeared perfectly perpendicular.

"What is that?" he asked, pointing. "Another tower?"

"No, not a tower, but a pillar," answered Dux. "The Pillar of Beauty. It is a marvel, isn't it? It's the height of twenty men, at least, and hewn from Parian marble. That's where we're headed. It marks the location of the South Gate."

"It must be a very important gate to merit such an enormous marker."

"Indeed. An impenetrable wall nearly half as tall as the pillar separates this, the civilized half of the southern realm, from an area known as the Southern Wilderness. We need to pass through that wilderness to reach the West. But first, we must pass through the South Gate, which is guarded by a powerful Warden."

Gaius slowed and turned his head toward his guide. "But he will let us pass through the gate, won't he?"

"I don't know. My guess is that he'll ask you a lot of questions before deciding that."

"Questions? What kind of questions? I know nothing of this world."

"I'll answer for you, when possible. Just stay at my side, and only speak to him if he speaks to you."

"But what if he will not let us pass?"

"Then our journey is at an end."

Gaius's heart sank. "Is there no other road? No way around the wall?"

"None," said Dux, shaking his head. "The South Gate is the only way."

Disheartened at the prospect of being turned back so early in his journey, Gaius slogged forward without further comment, his mind flooded with worry, until his ruminations were violently interrupted.

BOOM!

The unexpected explosion was so loud that Gaius recoiled and almost fell to the ground, his hands over his ears. With the sound still echoing through distant hills, he looked at Dux pleadingly and said, "What is that?"

"A signal cannon. The firing of the cannon notifies the residents of the many realms that travelers are nearing the South Gate."

"The cannon can be heard in other realms?"

"Oh yes. It echoes from here to the far corners of the world – East, West, and North. You have heard its force. Does that surprise you?"

"No," admitted Gaius. "It is exceedingly loud."

The two men now arrived at a long, wide yard with marble statues erected on the left and right sides. There were dozens of statues of men, women, animals, and strange creatures, some historical and some mythological. They faced the path on which Gaius and his guide traveled.

"What are these?" asked the initiate, marveling at the exquisite craftsmanship.

"These are the heroes and heroines of the realm," answered his guide. He pointed at several sculptures on the left side of the road. "Those are the mortals: Helen of Troy, Phryne, Bathsheba, Salome, and so forth." He moved his hand. "And on this side, the immortal or mythological heroes: Aphrodite, Hebe, Venus, Voluptas, Adonis, and so on."

"There are so many!"

"Yes, beauty takes many forms and every culture contributes its own idols. The ones along this path are the best known, but there is a magnificent field a few miles from here that hosts at least ten thousand such statues."

Gaius stopped in front of the statue of Aphrodite. It was uncannily realistic. Her marble flesh was so finely conceived that it even had pores. She wore what many of the ancient gods and goddesses wore, which was not much, if the realm's artists were to be trusted. Gaius found himself blushing under her stony gaze.

"If only such beauty was real..." he said in a low breath.

"Do you think it isn't?"

"No. It's too perfect."

"If an artist can conceive it, and you can appreciate it, the beauty is real," offered Dux. "But come along now. We are not tourists."

Gaius forced his eyes away from the beautiful Aphrodite and back to the path. The men proceeded down the corridor of heroes for another ten minutes until they reached the titanic Pillar of Beauty that marked the location of the South Gate.

The pillar was, Gaius guessed, six feet in diameter and thirty feet tall, at least. He observed that there was a series of vertical, concave grooves spaced equally around the perimeter of the pillar, each the width of a flute. They extended from the base to the capital.

"What are these grooves called?" the traveler asked. "The ones that look like a flute was pressed into wet clay?"

"Fluting," replied his guide.

"You say that in jest?"

"No. I am serious. They're called flutings."

"Oh." Gaius strained his neck to examine the capital, or top, of the pillar. He spotted what he thought might be a fanciful marble flower pot, from which emerged large leaves, or perhaps husks, and what he thought might be hibiscus flowers. The pillar's capital appeared to support the very canopy of the heavens.

Dux said, "It's impressive, isn't it? The legend is that this pillar was inspired by a beautiful woman carrying a basket on her head."

His spell only partially broken, Gaius mumbled, "She must have been very thin."

"Pardon?"

"I mean, if she were the height of a normal woman, but had the same proportions as the Pillar of Beauty, would be quite thin, I think. What was her name?"

Dux ignored the rather inane comment about the legendary woman's proportions, instead focusing on his charge's question. He saw a way to use it to his advantage. "Corinthia. *Corinthia the Thin.* She had this odd habit of walking around with a flower pot on her head. Do you understand?"

Gaius lowered his eyes and gave his guide an empty look. "What?"

Dux sighed. "Corinthia-the-thin. *Corinthian.*" He motioned at the pillar. "This is a Corinthian pillar."

Gaius made a face. "Obviously. It's named after her."

"No," replied his guide. "*Corinthian* is an order of architecture. There was no woman by that name. I said that in order to give you a way to memorize the word *Corinthian*."

"Oh! Corinthia the Thin, with a flower pot on her head." Gaius blushed. "*Corinthian*. Yes, understand now."

Dux did not seem convinced, but he said, "Good. Now, let us continue our trek. Once we get past the pillar, and nearer the wall, you'll see the gate. Don't worry, there will be plenty of opportunities for you to study the pillar later."

Gaius trotted forward, catching up to his guide, and then charged ahead of him, so eager was he to see the South Gate. It was a hundred paces ahead and the traveler, being young and fast, reached it quickly.

The gate was even more beautiful than he'd expected. It consisted of two interlocked sections, or doors, each five feet in width and twenty feet in height. The gate consisted of thick, spiraling posts, set five inches apart, made from gold and silver, which were held in place by five platinum rails. Both the posts and rails were studded with colorful jewels of every variety.

A wall extended on either side of the gate as far as the eye could see. It was constructed of white granite blocks so finely carved and placed that there was no mortar evident in the joints, and so perfectly polished that Gaius was forced to avert their eyes for fear of being blinded by the sun's reflection.

Then came the challenge: "Who are you, and why are you here?"

CHAPTER 4

THE WARDEN OF THE SOUTH

Gaius pivoted left to discover a man standing only a few feet away. He was tall and lean and wore an immaculate and unblemished suit of white metal armor, minus the helmet. There was a curious vertical bar, resembling an "I," carved into the breastplate. The man was remarkably handsome, with a finely sculpted face, piercing emerald eyes, and golden hair.

Behind him was a large chair, from which he had apparently just risen. It had a high, elaborately carved back, equally elaborate arms, and a blue velvet seat. It was made of some exotic wood Gaius had never seen before.

There was a bronze plate affixed to the top of the chair on which was engraved the words HIGH NOON.

"Greetings, Warden," said Dux, coming nearer. "This is Gaius. He is a friend from the land of darkness. Now that he is of age, he would like to join our order. He hopes to learn what we have to teach and to join us in our search for knowledge. I am taking him to meet the Master."

The handsome Warden looked at Dux, crossed his arms, and arched an eyebrow. "Is that so?" He shifted his glance to Gaius.

Gaius, not sure if he was supposed to reply, mumbled, "Yes, sir."

The warden grunted, as if displeased. "I'd advise you to reconsider." He and motioned toward the massive South Gate. "The road beyond this gate is long and treacherous. It is rarely traveled, and there's a reason for that. Are you doing this on a dare?"

"No, sir."

"No? Then you are trying to impress your friends, I think." The Warden walked behind Gaius and leaned in, saying in a low, conspiratorial, tone, "Or is it a girl? Every maiden loves a man in armor. I wouldn't blame you for that. But there are easier ways to win her hand, I assure you."

"That's not it, sir."

The Warden circled back around to stand directly in front of Gaius. "Then I can only assume someone has sent you here to learn our Order's secrets. You'll not get them, though. Many men have tried, and all have failed. You would turn around now, if you knew what's good for you."

Frustrated, Gaius shook his head. "On my honor, sir, no one has persuaded me to come here. It was my decision, and mine alone. I have no secret purpose."

The Warden studied the newcomer's face, checking for any untruth, then pivoted to face Dux. "You believe him?"

"I do. By all accounts, he's a well-respected lad in his village, and he is said to be upright before God. His ambitions are pure and meritorious."

The Warden considered this and seemed to relax ever-so-slightly. "But is he ready for what lies ahead? My guess is that his enthusiasm outweighs his ability. The beauty on this side of the gate is good and pure, but the beauty on the other side is untamed and dangerous. Your charge is rather, well...scrawny. It would be better if he waited another year or two. Bring him back then, when he is better prepared, and I will reconsider."

Gaius was about to object when his guide said, "I can assure you, Warden, that he has been properly prepared for what lies ahead."

The Warden moved his jaw left and right as if chewing on the words. "If I let you pass, where will you two go?"

"Through the southern wilderness to the West Gate, and then, further, into the northern wilderness."

The Warden grunted and shook his head. "I do not understand. Why would you go west when there is so much beauty to be found here, in my realm? And why continue from there to the north, where this nothing but darkness and confusion?" He cocked his head to one side, looking again at Gaius, but speaking to Dux. "I should warn you that there is no turning back if I let you pass. This gate is an exit, not an entrance. Once you and your companion are on the other side, and this gate is at your backs, your only available direction is forward. I am forbidden from opening this gate to anyone who approaches it from the other side, no matter how desperate the pleas."

Dux nodded. "Of that, I am aware. I will be with our friend every step of the way. So long as he stays by my side, he will be safe."

The Warden lifted his chin slightly. "The knights who found this man worthy – do I know them?"

"Yes. They are men you trust."

"And they believe he is qualified to join us?"

"More than that. They recommend him."

"I see," responded the Warden quietly. He put his gloved hands on his armored hips and began to pace, shaking his head slowly as he did so.

Gaius was concerned. Despite his guide responding smartly to every challenge made by the Warden, the guardian of the South Gate seemed determined to prevent any man from passing through it.

So he was surprised when the Warden stopped pacing and turned to face both visitors. There was the hint of a smile on his lips. "You seem to have exhausted all my objections, Brother."

"And good ones they were," responded Dux. "But, in fairness, they rarely change. You've become rather predictable."

The Warden laughed. He moved toward Dux and the men embraced. "Very well. I will allow you to pass. Good to see you again, Brother Dux."

The guide replied, "Good to see you, also, Warden."

When the men stepped away from one another, the Warden looked back and forth between Gaius and Dux, saying, "Is there anything you need?"

"May we rest here for awhile? We've been on our feet since before the sun rose."

"Of course," answered the Warden, motioning toward a soft patch of grass nearby. His countenance had changed dramatically. He now exhibited nothing but civility and kindness. "Sit and take a break from your labors. Would you care for any refreshments? Water, perhaps? Wine?"

"Wine would be excellent, thank you. But can you spare any? We don't want to take advantage of your generosity."

"Oh, yes, I have wine to spare. Since you and I last met, I've had to restrict the amount of wine allotted to the locals. They're an artistic bunch, as you know, and many of them drink in search of 'inspiration.' I don't necessarily agree with that approach, but a little wine does no harm. Unfortunately, a few of our citizens have been known to drink in excess, at which point they inevitably get into loud arguments about who is the greatest painter, musician, or poet, or who is more handsome or beautiful, and so on, and became so dizzy from drink that they can't sit or stand uprightly. There is a group of actors that hang about a grove of plum trees that have been a particular issue."

"You've reduced their allotment of wine, then?"

"Yes. Each day at noon, I set out a few barrels in a field below and call the citizens to refreshment. I monitor them to make sure none overindulge, and after an hour has passed, I have the barrels removed and send everyone back to their labors. They've become much more productive since I implemented this policy."

"That must please the Master."

"It does. It has also resulted in my having an excess of wine available."

Dux shrugged. "Since this wise policy has left you with an excess of that glorious elixir, I would be very happy to accept a cup from you."

"And your charge?"

"Water for him, if you please." Dux gave Gaius an apologetic look. "Sorry, my friend, but at this point, it's best that you keep your wits about you. We've got a long road ahead of us."

Gaius and his guide were just finishing their refreshments when they were jolted by a sudden flash of light, as if a bolt of lightning had struck nearby. There was a clap of thunder.

"Is it the end of the world?" asked Gaius.

"Not quite," answered the Warden, who was looking toward the sun. "But I suspect we have a visitor from a place very near there."

A moment later, a dove descended from the sky. It landed, flickered, and was replaced by the form of a man. The man was young – perhaps even younger than Gaius - and had the lean, muscular body of a marathon runner. He wore an odd type of leather armor, white in color, which seemed to cling to his body. He carried a long rod similar to the one carried by Dux, though it was capped by something that resembled a ram's horn. In his other hand, the man held a scroll sealed with wax.

The newcomer's most striking feature was his helmet, which looked like an inverted silver bowl with wings on either side. At the front was a device that resembled a crescent moon. He removed it and placed it under one arm as he turned to face the Warden.

"Diakonos," said the Warden to the arrival, taking a step forward. "Your appearance is untimely. I have company, as you can see."

The man named Diakonos glanced at Gaius, then his guide, before returning his gaze to the Warden. "My apologies, Brother, but I carry a message from the west." He extended the scroll.

The Warden accepted it and began breaking the wax with his fingers. As he did so, he grumbled, to no one in particular, "This had better be important."

Gaius saw that his guide had risen and was beginning to assemble his meager belongings. He sensed that the time had come to pass through the South Gate, so he did the same. By the time the two were ready, the Warden had finished reading the contents of the scroll.

He looked at Dux, his expression grave. "News from King Solomon. Hiram Abiff has disappeared."

"Disappeared?"

The warden nodded. "He failed to appear at the worksite yesterday."

Dux's expression was grave. "He's the most dependable man in the world. If he needed to leave the worksite for some reason, he'd have told King Solomon in advance, and obtained his permission."

"As you say. The hope is he wandered into the nearby hills to rest, or in search of inspiration. He could have easily become lost." The warden glanced again at the scroll. "King Solomon requests that any sightings of Hiram be reported to him immediately..." His voice trailed off

"Is there something else?"

The Warden appeared circumspect, and Gaius realized that there were things the warden wanted to say, but couldn't, because of his presence. Looking back at Dux, the Warden said, "There is something else missing. Something of great value."

Gaius looked anxiously at his guide, hoping the man would ask what this "something else" was. There was clearly a great mystery evolving.

But his guide's only response was, "You'll want to attend to this matter immediately, of course. We'll be on our way. Thank you for your hospitality, Brother. I promise to keep my eyes open."

CHAPTER 5

THE SOUTHERN WILDERNESS

Gaius watched with trepidation as the South Gate was closed behind him, mindful of the Warden's warning that there was no turning back. The wall on this side was much like the wall on the other, but the sun now seemed a little off-center and its rays weren't reflected by the polished blocks. Looking up, Gaius could still see the cyclopean Pillar of Beauty towering above him, though its base was hidden behind the wall.

He was surprised to find the land on this side of the South Gate almost identical to the land on the other. The hills seemed a bit steeper, and he could see clouds in the far distance, but the air was still fragrant and the flowers still abundant.

"This is not so bad," he said to his companion. "What makes this part of the southern realm any more dangerous than the one we came from?"

"The creatures and people who live here," responded his guide, already moving down the path and away from the gate.

Gaius hurried to catch up. "What is wrong with the people?"

"There is no Warden on this side of the wall, and as a result, the people are given to excess and indulgence. They lack the virtue of temperance."

"You mean there is no law on this side of the wall?"

"Only the most primitive kind. Stay close and follow my instructions. We'll travel until sunset, and by then, with any luck, we'll have reached the West Gate."

Gaius was confused. "Is this world so small? How is it that we can travel from the southern edge of the world to the western edge in such a short amount of time?"

"We are not traveling from edge to edge, but rather around the center. Imagine that the world is a wheel – a circle, with a point in the center. We are not traveling along the circumference of the wheel. We are traveling around the spoke that holds the wheel in place."

"So, the world like a wheel?"

"In a way, yes. And the outer edge of the wheel is like a boundary line."

"What's on the other side of the boundary line?"

"Evil," his guide replied. "Great evil. And death."

"What does the boundary line look like? Is it a stone wall, like the one at the South Gate?"

"No. It is, unfortunately, invisible. A man might easily step across the line without realizing it. But you need not worry. Though invisible, the boundary line is easily detected by a man with a pure heart. So long as you are good, keeping your passions in check, treating others fairly, and living unselfishly, there is no chance you'll accidentally cross over. If you wander too close, your heart and mind will warn you to move in the opposite direction."

Gaius weighed this advice before saying, "Do you think Hiram Abiff accidentally crossed the boundary line?"

"No," replied Dux firmly. "He has one of the purest hearts in all the world."

"But..."

"Yes?"

"Well, it sounded to me as if he might have stolen something from King Solomon. The Warden said-"

"I know what the Warden said, and I can understand why you'd make that inference, but I promise you, our brother, Hiram, has stolen nothing. The thing which is missing was given to Hiram long ago. He carried it with him, always. Consequently, when he disappeared, it was lost with him."

"Oh," said Gaius, regretting his insinuation that the noble Hiram Abiff – a member of the very Order which he, himself, hoped to join – had committed a crime. "Perhaps I can help you and the others in your search?"

Dux gave him a weak smile. "Yes, perhaps. At some point. But for now, you must complete your journey with me."

Gaius, ever inquisitive, was about to ask Dux why the guide was escorting him *around* the spoke of the world's wheel, as opposed to just crossing from one side to another, but he lost his train of thought when he saw a woman approaching. She was very near, and Gaius wondered how he had not seen her coming.

"Greetings," she said when she was but a few paces away. Her voice was lyrical, sultry, and sweet.

"Hello," replied Gaius, his heart skipping a beat. The woman was impossibly beautiful, with an exquisite form, vexing eyes, luscious lips, high cheekbones, and unblemished flesh. When Gaius smelled her perfume, he came very near to fainting.

"You're a handsome one," the woman said, tilting her head to one side and letting her long, golden hair fall across a bare shoulder. She was dressed in a sheer, sleeveless garment that dropped to mid-thigh. It telegraphed every underlying curve. "What is your name?"

It took several seconds for Gaius to find his voice. He stuttered. "G-G-G...*Gaius*."

She took a step closer. "Gaius. What a splendid name. I have known many men by that name, and all were extraordinary...just like you. Welcome to my home." She twirled slowly in place, her arms floating in the air. "My beautiful, wonderful home."

The woman stopped spinning and advanced until her body was an inch from the young traveler's. She pushed her lower lip forward, as if pouting. "But it is so lonely, being here alone..."

"You? Alone?" Gaius couldn't imagine how that was possible.

"Yes," the woman said. She sniffled and placed a delicate hand against his chest. "All alone. Perhaps...perhaps you might stay awhile, and keep me company?"

The sensation of the woman's fingers caused goosebumps to erupt on Gaius's skin. "I would, um..." He wiped at his brow. "I would like to...very much." He thought his heart might explode. "But I...well, you see...there is something I need to do at this moment. Something important."

The woman frowned and lowered her eyes. "Is it really so important? More important than me?"

"No...I mean, yes...but..." He looked at this guide, who had been oddly silent until now.

Dux said, "Where is your husband, Aphrodite?"

The woman's body froze, but her eyes dropped and shifted left. "Husband?"

"Yes. I think you know him? *Hephaestus.*"

There was an awkward pause. Finally, she mumbled, "He is no longer my husband. Not really."

"Oh?"

The woman took a step back and faced the older man. "He abandoned me. He's in the West, plying his trade among the builders." She shrugged again. "He never really appreciated me. With him, it's always work, work, work."

She glanced back at Gaius and smiled. "But here is a man who truly appreciates beauty. I'm sure of it. You do, don't you?"

Gaius nodded. "Of course, but-"

"Stay with me, Gaius, and I will show you so many wonderful things! At my palace, I have the best wine and the best food and the best musicians in all the world. Your every desire will be satisfied ten-fold. You will experience joys that you never believed possible. The beauty of this land is unlimited."

She took a step back and frowned. "I can see from your posture and countenance that you are one of those upright men who spend too much time on *important things*. You need to loosen up, Gaius."

"That's enough of that," said Dux loudly. "Find another fly for your web. This one has places to go."

The woman retreated a step, her face now painted with contempt. "Let the boy decide," she seethed. For a split second, her great beauty was replaced by something more sinister – something terrible.

She regained her composure quickly, however, and the seductive smile returned. The woman extended a delicate hand toward Gaius. "All you need to do is bow to me. Just lower your head and kiss my hand. That's all it takes. Then I will be yours, and you will be mine."

Gaius, tempted, closed his eyes but remained upright. "I'm sorry, no. I can't stay here. As you say, I have important things to do."

He heard Dux say, "There's your answer, Temptress. Slither back to your garden. This traveler will not succumb to your charms today."

There was a sound, like the roar of a great wind, and Gaius opened his eyes.

The woman was gone.

"Good riddance," said Dux.

After taking a few seconds to collect himself, Gaius said, "Was that really Aphrodite?"

"No, it was only one aspect of her. The best and worst aspect, if you take my meaning."

"Would she have killed me?"

Dux laughed. "No, that's not her style. She would have given you exactly what she promised, and for that reason, you would have never escaped this place. You see, time has a way of passing more quickly here. You look in the mirror one morning and find your skin smooth and unwrinkled, your hair thick, and your eyes full of life. A few days pass, or seem to, and you notice wrinkles, and bumps, and bald spots. A few days after that-" The guide snapped his fingers. "And you're an old man. Most who succumb to Aphrodite die here, in the Southern Wilderness, never realizing they are a prisoner.

He bobbled his head right and left. "Of course, some men do break her spell, in time. Sadly, those poor souls are usually far past their prime and awake quite disoriented. They are surprised at how much time has passed and aren't sure what to do. They usually wander in a daze to the South Gate, and there plead for the Warden to open it."

"But the Warden told us that no one can return through the South Gate."

"Just so. Consequently, those who have their wits about them and an inkling regarding how the sun moves will find their way to the West Gate, but most lack the strength necessary to survive the journey. The West is not very hospitable to old men."

"Is every traveler who passes this way tempted by Aphrodite?"

"No. The temptation varies according to the person. A young man like yourself will attract a creature like Aphrodite, or Venus, or Jezebel, or some other temptress. But those who have a great love of music typically fall victim to the Sirens. Those who are vain are attracted to certain sprites that lurk in the creeks, rivers, and ponds and appear as their victims' reflections, though much improved. Ironically, the travelers who succumb to those creatures die of thirst because they forget the need to drink the water that is right in front of them!"

Gaius now realized how lucky he had been. "Is there a lesson to be learned here?"

"Yes," said his guide, "there is. Are you familiar with the four cardinal virtues?"

Gaius nodded. "Temperance, Fortitude, Prudence, and Justice."

"Very good. You'll find that each of them plays a role in keeping you safe as you pass through the gates. The first, for example, is Temperance, a value you will find particularly helpful in the untamed beauty of the Southern Wilderness. Tell me what Temperance is."

Gaius thought for a moment. "Self-control, I'd say. The ability to control your desires and not over-indulge."

"That's right," agreed his guide. "It is a reasonable restraint upon our affections and passions. It prevents us from indulging in excesses or picking up licentious or vicious habits."

"Licentious?"

"Promiscuous. You can see, then, how Temperance can save you from creatures such as Aphrodite."

"Yes. But what of Fortitude, Prudence, and Justice? Are they not applicable here?"

Dux shrugged. "They are all applicable everywhere, my friend, yet you'll find that one is more pertinent than the others in each realm. In this realm, Temperance is the most pertinent, for the reasons we just discussed."

"But surely temperance does not apply to all beautiful and enjoyable things. Music, for example. How can beautiful music ever be bad?"

Dux frowned. "Many men have committed atrocities inspired by the beat of a drum. Others have been so driven to despair by a sad song that they've taken their own lives, or the lives of loved ones. On a whole, of course, music is a wonderful thing, but it also has a hypnotic quality, and it is common for wicked men to wrap their words in music to make their evils palatable, or even desirable."

Gaius pondered this. "But what of artwork? Surely, a beautiful painting cannot be-"

"Whether it is beautiful is subjective," interrupted Dux. "But consider that the pursuit of ideal beauty may cause a man to overlook the many 'lesser' beauties all around him, which would otherwise bring him happiness. Every man cannot be Adonis, nor every woman Venus. Consider also that an artist may seek to denigrate some person, culture, or value, by falsely demonstrating how beautiful the alternative is. This is called propaganda."

He raised a finger in the air. "Again, do not mistake my meaning. I am a great lover of beauty and a promoter of both music and art. I seek only to demonstrate that temperance allows you to enjoy the benefits of beauty in a thoughtful manner."

"I understand."

"Very good. You did well, my friend. You showed restraint and remained steady and upright when confronted with a very great temptation. That bodes well for the rest of your journey."

"Thank you, sir."

Dux nodded and began moving down the path. "Let's continue our journey."

THE REALM OF STRENGTH

The remainder of the duo's trek through the Southern Wilderness was uneventful. The land all around them remained spectacularly beautiful. They passed through an area that was populated by aromatic cedars, another with bubbling creeks and tiny, picturesque waterfalls, and yet another with strange, glowing trees which hosted several peculiar species of giant, colorful birds.

But as the hours passed, the beauty began to slowly diminish. The land became more barren and the air become warmer and less fragrant. The sun raced ahead of them so that they were walking toward it instead of underneath it, and the sky was transformed from bright blue to purplish pink. Some stars appeared, and a crescent moon, and crickets began to chirp on either side of the path.

Dux pointed. "The village ahead falls under the purview of the Warden of the West."

Gaius scanned the horizon and saw a grid of squat stone structures that resembled oversized bricks. Each was shaped like an inverted "T," with a single doorway, a single window, and a single, oversized chimney in the center. Abutting each door was a lighted torch.

"Why are all the buildings so drab?" Gaius asked.

"The people here have a different temperament than those in the South. They value strength above all other things. The buildings you see are remarkably sturdy. The blocks used to construct the walls are a foot thick. The roofs are supported by iron beams. Come back in a thousand years, and these buildings will still be here, exactly as you see them today."

"But why are they identical?"

"Well, unlike the citizens of the southern realm, the northern people view beauty as both superfluous and transitory. What they want are functionality and dependability. Consequently, if something has been proven to work, they stick with it. Their houses are identical because they're based on the same dependable, centuries-old design."

The guide pointed to a place beyond the village. "But look there! Do you see it? A far more impressive structure: the Pillar of Strength."

Gaius raised his chin. In the distance, below the purple sky, and silhouetted against the cool orange rays of the setting sun, was a pillar equal in height to the Pillar of Beauty, but wider and sturdier in appearance.

"I see it," he said, duly impressed. "Does it mark the location of the West Gate?"

"It does."

The two walked until they reached the village of squat buildings. The dull glow of candles radiated through the cracks of the shuttered windows, and smoke rose from the elongated chimneys. Gaius could smell food being cooked. His stomach growled.

"It appears everyone has returned home for the day," he said. "What are the vocations of the people here?"

Dux moved his staff from his left to his right hand. "The people of the West are hard-working and industrious. Some of the world's greatest metal workers, armorers, and blacksmiths reside here. A number of others work in mines, rock quarries, and on farms. If a job requires strength, endurance, and sweat, you'll find it in the western realm."

Gaius spotted two men talking nearby. They wore studded leather tunics, wool trousers, and boots. Both were huge - easily a foot taller than Gaius - with broad chests and shoulders, and bulging muscles. Their faces seemed to be chiseled from stone.

He whispered to his guide, "I don't think I'd want to run afoul of such men."

"No, you wouldn't," agreed Dux. "But don't worry. Though they appear intimidating, most of the residents are civil and peace-loving. They live simple and honest lives. They rise with the sun, work hard all day, and go home just before sunset. They use their strength to build, not to destroy."

The travelers walked for another hour, following the path in the direction of the setting sun, passing many houses and storefronts. The stores looked much like the houses, only larger. None were open for business.

"There are no night owls here," Gaius observed.

"Early to bed, early to rise," replied Dux.

Yet on the outskirts of the village, they found one man still working. He resembled the men Gaius had spotted in the village, the only difference being that this man was bare-chested and covered in sweat. He stood before a forge and was striking a sheet of hot, glowing metal with a hammer. Behind him was a kiln that radiated a fierce heat.

When he saw the two men approaching, the worker set his hammer down and walked toward them, wiping his hands on a white cloth that was tied around his waist. He looked at Dux and smiled. "Greetings, Brother. It's been a long time."

"At least three moons," agreed the guide, shaking a proffered hand. "Still working the night shift, I see."

The man laughed. "And the day shift, and every other shift." He looked at Gaius. "What is your name, young man?"

"Gaius, sir."

"Pleased to meet you, Gaius."

"I'm pleased to meet you, sir," Gaius replied, noticing that the man had not offered his own name. "You are a blacksmith?"

"Not exactly. I'm an artificer."

Dux, seeing Gaius's incomprehension, said, "An artificer is a… well, a maker of original things; things of that only the most clever and cunning man could conceive of. He's simultaneously a blacksmith, chemist, metallurgist, and inventor, and is perhaps most famous for his pioneering work with brass."

Gaius bowed slightly. "I've never met an…uh, an arf-ti-ce-fer before."

The might man laughed. "Neither have I! The word is *artificer*, my friend. As in *artifact* or *artificial*."

"Doesn't *artificial* mean fake?"

"No. It means manmade - something produced by human hands instead of nature."

"Oh," said Gaius, embarrassed. "I didn't mean to imply-"

"No offense taken."

"You live here, then? In the West?"

"I spend a lot of my time here, yes, but I also spend time in the South. I've got what you could call 'dual-citizenship.' In the South, the people prefer form over function, and here, in the West, they prefer function over form. Me, I want both. There's no reason armor and weaponry, for example, can't be strong and beautiful."

Gaius motioned toward the forge. "What are you working on today?"

"A very specialized form of armor. It's made of a metal that is virtually impenetrable."

"I wonder how you can shape such metal into armor if it is as strong as you say."

The man shrugged. "I use the best charcoal in my furnace. Used in the proper amount and lit properly, even the most obdurate metals will yield to it. Even this new metal." Seeing Gaius's confusion, he said, "*Obdurate* means inflexible, my friend. Unbending."

"Oh," replied Gaius.

The man chuckled and looked at Dux. "My apologies, but I do need to get back to work. The metal is cooling."

"Of course," said Dux, taking Gaius gently by the arm. "We'll be on our way. It was good to see you again, Brother."

The two travelers continued on their way, and when they were some half-mile past the artificer, there was a loud BOOM from an unseen, but very near, cannon.

This time, Gaius winced only slightly. "That is the signal that we are approaching the West Gate."

"Just so," replied Dux.

A few minutes later, the two men arrived at a long yard lined by statues on either side. It was exactly like the one the men had encountered in the South, except that the statues here were of different people and mythological creatures.

"Are these the heroes of the West?" asked Gaius.

"Yes." Dux nodded toward the statues on the left. "You'll recognize a few of them. Hercules, for example, is just there, and further down you'll see a statue of Samson. Many of the heroes on the mortal side are famous warriors, though there are also some merchants and builders. That statue, for example, depicts the King of Tyre."

Gaius looked at the statue of the king. The man was not physically impressive, though the garments he wore were those of a regent. "He does not look like the other people of the West."

"You've only met a few of them, Gaius. Strength comes in many forms. It can be physical, but it might be military, diplomatic, or monetary. The King of Tyre is strong because he is a wealthy and powerful ruler."

Gaius motioned at another statue of an elderly man wearing clothing of a kind he'd never seen. "Who is this?"

"Ah, yes," said Dux, crossing his arms. "Him. He was an abbot. Curious fellow, and very smart, but rather a two-dimensional thinker, in my opinion. A good brother, nonetheless." He gestured at the statues on the other side of the path. "These are the immortal heroes of the West - Kratos, Nike, Bia, Zelus, Magni, Plutus, and so on."

Gaius was unfamiliar with most of the names, but he knew there would be time later to research them. There were a great number of statues and he couldn't expect Dux to give a history of each of the men, women, and creatures whom they depicted.

Eventually, the two travelers reached the foot of the hill on which the Pillar of Strength had been erected. Though just as massive, it was simpler than the Pillar of Beauty. There were no leaves or plants at the top. Instead, there was a flat, round section that resembled a coin lying flat, on top of which was a square board of about the same thickness. The pillar was the same height as the Pillar of Beauty and fluted in the same manner, but it was noticeably thicker.

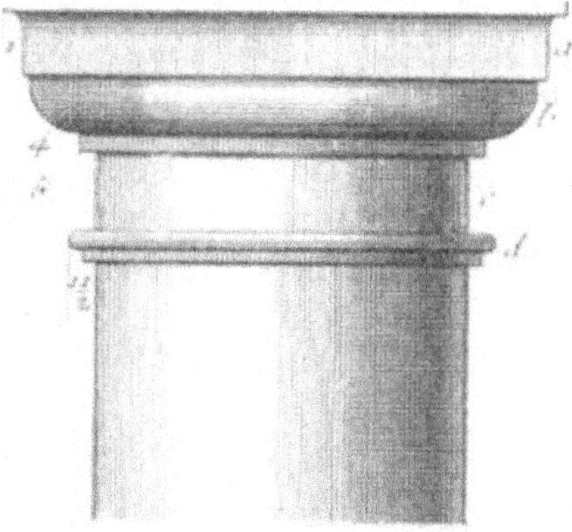

"It's formidable, I admit," said Gaius, "but not as ornate as the Pillar in the South."

Dux replied, "This pillar represents function over form. In the West, it's the strength of the pillar that matters, not its beauty."

"Who was this pillar named after?" asked Gaius.

His guide was ready for the question. "A man named Icarus, better known as just 'Ick' because he loathed bathing. He was a huge man and a soldier whose specialty was knocking down even the largest and heaviest of castle doors with a battering ram that looked remarkably like this pillar. That's why it's so plain and flat on top. Because of his strength, Ick was greatly admired here in the West. Would you like to guess as to this pillar's architectural order?"

Gaius thought for a moment. "Ick-door?"

"Close. Door-ick. *Doric*."

Gaius tugged at his lower lip. "You made up the story about a giant named Icarus, right?"

"Yes."

"And the whole door thing–"

"Yes, I made that up, also. Listen, when trying to remember something in a field that doesn't appeal to you, or which you can't quite grasp, you must find a way to make the subject more interesting. An order of architecture may not interest you, but a giant who doesn't bathe and who can pound open doors with a battering ram that resembles this pillar does. Do you understand?"

"Yes," said Gaius earnestly.

"Good. Let us continue to the West Gate."

CHAPTER 7

THE WARDEN OF THE WEST

As they continued up the hill, a man strode past them, apparently on his way back to the village. He gripped a large canvas bag against his chest. The top was tied shut, but there was a tiny hole at the bottom of the bag, and from it dropped a few kernels of dried corn. Noticing this, the man moved a hand to cover the hole and move forward with increased urgency.

Gaius said, "Why was that man carrying a bag of corn?"

"He has just been paid."

"The people here are paid in corn?"

"Yes, just as the citizens of the South are paid in wine. Westerners don't consume wine because they feel it makes them less productive. But they prize corn because it gives them energy to perform their work."

"Today is payday, then?"

"Every day is payday in the West. It's the custom here to pay each man the wages he is due at the end of the day. The man you saw was descending from the West Gate because the Warden of the West is responsible for paying the workers."

"Really? Why is that his responsibility?"

His guide moved his head left and right. "Well, it's complicated. You see, the people here are hardworking and proud, and, for their efforts, they demand a level playing field. If a man believes he has not been paid what he's due, there will be unrest. If a man believes that another worker has been paid more than him, for doing the same work - again, there will be unrest. Everyone here trusts the Warden to be fair and evenhanded, so it's only natural that he should be the paymaster. The satisfaction of the workers is necessary to maintain harmony, which is quite important in this society."

"Harmony is important in *all* societies," observed Gaius.

"Yes," agreed his guide, raising a finger into the air, "but it is especially important in this one."

"So, the Warden here is responsible for both paying the workers their daily wages and guarding the West Gate?"

"More than that. He also does a lot of work for the Master, and when the Master is unavailable, the Warden will usually take on his duties, also."

The two walked for another few minutes before at last reaching the West Gate and the wall that encased it. The wall had the same dimensions as the wall in the South, but its blocks were granite instead of marble. The blocks were unpolished, the minerals that composed the granite being predominantly gray and black. Instead of reflecting light, the western wall seemed to absorb it, though there was little light to be had from the setting sun.

The West Gate was two seemingly impenetrable door fabricated from thick oak planks that were bound tightly together by a series of sturdy, inch-thick iron rails. Each door of the gate was ten feet wide and ten feet tall, making the gate's width twice its height when the doors were closed. Gaius thought the doors might have once painted red, but the paint had faded, and the oak planks now had but a rusty hue.

On the left side of the gate was a hill of bags filled with corn. There were kernels of corn almost everywhere – on the path, around the Pillar of Strength, near the West Gate, and everywhere in-between.

On the right side of the gate was a gargantuan chair that resembled, more than anything else, a throne, with a high back, wide, thick arms, and tiger claw feet. It had a red velvet cushion on the seat. There was a bronze plate affixed to the top of the chair on which was engraved a single word: DUSK.

A giant sat in the chair, and Gaius understood immediately that he was the Warden of the West. The Warden was the largest and most intimidating man Gaius had ever seen. Though the man was sitting, Gaius guessed that he was at least eight feet tall and half as broad at the shoulders. The man's thick upper torso was protected by white scale mail. A horizontal bar, like a dash, was carved into the cuirass at chest level. The man's ridiculously large biceps, just discernible beneath a red cloak, were circumscribed by studded leather straps.

He was perhaps in his fourth decade, with a full, bushy black beard that fell below his neck. His tanned, scarred flesh had the texture of burlap and the shape of the man's nose suggested it had been broken more than once. Yet his brown eyes were alert and hinted at a keen intellect.

"Who are you?" the giant asked in a deep and powerful voice. The air shimmered.

Gaius instinctively took a step backward but was steadied by his guide.

"Greetings, Warden," said Dux. "This is -"

"Ah, yes," interrupted the Warden, waving a ham-sized hand and standing. He towered over both visitors. Looking at Dux, he said, "I know who this is. Diakonos returned from the South not long ago and told me of your travels. This is the young man who wishes to join our Order, is that right?"

"It is," replied the guide.

"Hmph," grunted the Warden, scratching the flesh beneath his beard. He examined the traveler with skepticism. "He's a skinny one..."

The Warden stepped forward, circled Gaius and, when he was again facing him, put a hand on the man's shoulder. "Listen, lad, the Warden in the South is young, and because of that, he is an optimist. Though he may seem a tough customer, the truth is that he thinks things will always work out for the best. He hasn't been trampled enough by the world to understand that sometimes things don't go as planned."

He pointed at the nearby gate with his free hand. "I've let many men pass through that gate who were never seen or heard from again. The Western Wilderness is a brutal place, and the northern realm beyond it is terrifying. I know that the Warden of the South examined you and found you worthy, and I know that if I asked you the same questions that he asked you, you and your guide would give me the same assurances that I should let you pass."

The Warden tightened his grip on Gaius's shoulder. "The road beyond is perilous, son. But if you tell me that you truly desire to pass, and cannot be deterred, I will open the gate."

Gaius swallowed hard and nodded. "I truly desire to pass, sir."

The Warden studied the young man's face for a moment, then put his hands on his waist. He looked at Dux and frowned. "Well...so be it. You have my permission to pass."

"Thank you," replied the guide. "But do you mind if we rest here for a short period?"

"Mind?" asked the Warden, all amazement. "I'd be insulted if you didn't, Brother. Look there," he said, pointing at a sturdy table just behind the tall pile of corn sacks. There were four oversized chairs around it. "That's my pay table, on that level area of ground. That's where I meet and pay the workers. I've just paid the last of them and was preparing to take my evening meal. Would you like to join me?"

"You're very kind, Warden. Yes, thank you."

The Warden slapped Dux on the back, nearly knocking him to the ground. "That's grand. Come along then. Tell me, do you like your corn raw, boiled, or fried?"

Their meal complete, the Warden said, "Yes, I'm worried about Hiram. He's not passed through here, nor the South, nor the East. The workers at the site think he's lost in the hills. I hope that's the case, but..."

He lowered his chin and leaned forward, toward Dux, who was sitting across from him. "In truth, I fear something worse has happened."

"Why is that?"

"I've heard that there are a number of workers missing from the site; men with poor reputations who were, unfortunately, recruited from villages very near the boundary line. Perhaps even beyond it."

Dux looked dubious. "Why would King Solomon employ such men?"

The Warden leaned back and splayed his hands. "There wasn't much choice, Brother. You know how many men are required to build the temple. Over a hundred and fifty thousand! When you're recruiting that many men, you're going to end up with some bad apples. King Hiram provided most of those workers, and did the best he could."

"King Hiram?" asked Gaius, astonished. "Hiram Abiff is a king?"

Dux shook his head. "No, Gaius. It's confusing, I realize, but there are two Hirams. Hiram Abiff, the artisan who has disappeared, and Hiram, the king Tyre. You recall seeing his statue earlier, do you not?"

"I do."

"As it happens, Hiram Abiff, the architect, was born in Tyre, which is ruled by King Hiram." He sighed. "I've never been there, but it seems to be an unwritten rule that all men from Tyre are named Hiram, and that if you meet a man named Hiram, he's from Tyre."

"The biggest difference between the two men," said the Warden, "is that Hiram, the king, is not an artisan. His primary interests are trade and commerce."

Dux said, "King Hiram was a friend of King Solomon's father, who was King David. Just before King David died, he instructed his son, Solomon, to build a great temple. Solomon wanted to comply, but lacked the manpower or know-how to carry out his late father's instructions."

The Warden said, "Fortunately, King Hiram came to the rescue, providing Solomon with both workers and materials. But he didn't have the luxury of interviewing every laborer he sent to Solomon's worksite. Nor should he have. Most of the men are apprentices whose only job is to turn large, ugly rocks into slightly smaller, less ugly blocks. It's hard but relatively simple work. Those crude blocks are improved by more skilled fellows, all craftsmen. Above the craftsman are a few thousand Master Masons."

"And at the very top of the pecking order," continued Dux, "are three men: King Solomon, King Hiram, and Hiram Abiff."

Gaius was surprised. "Hiram Abiff is so highly regarded that he keeps company with two kings?"

"Yes," answered his guide. "King Solomon's role is to wisely lead the temple's construction effort. King Hiram's role is to provide resources for its construction. Hiram Abiff's role is to make the temple beautiful. Remember, Solomon is erecting this temple to God. It must be magnificent."

He looked at the Warden. "I wonder if work on the temple has been suspended?"

"I would think so. Without a design on the trestle board, how will the workers know what to do?"

Dux scratched behind one ear, pondering the implications. "True. Well, thank you for the meal, Brother. We'll nap for a bit, then be on our way."

CHAPTER 8
THE WESTERN WILDERNESS

The West Gate closed behind the duo with a deafening thud. It was the final moments of dusk, so the only sources of light were the dying rays of the descending sun and the weak rays of the ascending moon. The sky was purple ahead of the two men and black behind them. Stars twinkled overhead. The land ahead consisted only of shadows. The sounds of owls, crickets, and nocturnal beings filled the air.

Gaius said, "I assume the perils of the Western Wilderness are more...physical?"

"Aphrodite wasn't physical enough for you?"

"I mean 'thump on the head' physical. The Pillar of West represents strength, after all."

"You're right. The attacks of the untamed creatures of the West are usually more brutal. There are tigers, bears, alligators, and so on, plus monsters of various types-"

"Monsters?"

"Yes. Some of them are so ineffable-"

"So what?"

"Ineffable."

Gaius shook his head. "What does that mean?"

"It means...well, it means a notch above incredible. Indescribable, even. The words sound alike, do they not? Ineffable and incredible?"

"Then why not say incredible?"

"Because something ineffable is even more incredible; so incredible that there are no words to fully describe it."

"Other than *ineffable*, you mean."

Dux frowned. "Anyway, focus on the 'eff' in ineffable. If you use your imagination, you can perhaps come up with some crude way of using that to help you remember what the word means."

Gaius thought for a moment, then brightened. "Oh! You mean-"

His guide held up a hand. "A word that need not be spoken."

"Oh," said Gaius again. "Of course."

Dux nodded. "Very well. As I was saying, there are monsters here in the Western Wilderness that are so ineffable that their appearance can induce heart attacks. Yet the most dangerous creatures here are the men. They have no scruples about capturing or killing any creature that crosses his path. There are scouts seeking slaves for barbarian kings, murderers, and robbers galore. Their insatiable hunger for power and riches leads to every imaginable cruelty."

Gaius surveyed the area around him. "That sounds far worse than the dangers we faced in the Southern Wilderness. What will we do to protect ourselves?"

"As long as we stay on this path, we should be fine. It was built straight and narrow and has been enchanted to repel those who desire to harm other living beings. If such a creature steps on this path, it – or he, or she - receives a very nasty, electrical shock."

"We will not be shocked?"

"No, for we intend no harm. We are merely travelers. But we must be careful. It's getting dark, and it will be easy to stray from the path if we're not careful."

"Do you have a torch?" asked Gaius.

"No," replied his Guide. "I've got something better."

The guide slammed the bottom of his staff into the ground three times and yelled, "Let there be light!"

And there was light. The emblem of the sun at the top of the staff began to glow, and that glow slowly increased until everything within a twenty-foot radius was illuminated.

Dux looked at his gaping charge and smiled. "Members of our Order never travel in darkness, Gaius. Not if we can avoid it."

Gaius said, "I am amazed, indeed! But..."

"Yes?"

"You didn't need to say that, did you? *Let there be light?* It was tapping the staff into the ground that activated the light, wasn't it?"

Dux sighed. "That's the problem with your generation. You don't appreciate a good show." He made a motion with his free hand. "Alright, let's go."

The two men moved forward. The first hour was uneventful, but toward the end of the second, both men heard a terrible grinding sound somewhere ahead of them. It was like the squeal of an unoiled hinge, only a thousand times louder. It was followed by the sound of an explosion. The earth trembled.

"What was that?" asked Gaius.

Dux didn't reply right away. "Perhaps a mine collapsed. There are several in the area."

But the grating sound returned, and the earth trembled again, this time more violently. The men waited for a few seconds longer, and when nothing else happened, they again began to advance, though cautiously.

Gaius said, "Is there a great pillar in the Western Wilderness?"

"A great pillar? Do you mean, like the Pillars of Beauty and Strength? No. Why do you ask?"

Gaius squinted at the far horizon, where the last remnants of the sun's rays formed a horizontal pink line. "I thought I saw one, further down the path. Maybe two."

"Two?"

Instead of replying, Gaius stopped moving and asked, "What are those two stars in the sky ahead of us? Both are red, and they are very close to one another. I thought I saw them..." His voice trailed off.

"Yes?"

"Well, I thought I saw them move."

At just that moment, the sound of metal scraping against metal again filled the air, and the earth shook again.

"There!" yelled Gaius. "You see? The stars moved!"

Dux looked, then let out a long breath. "Ah. This is not good."

"What? What's going on?"

The sound returned and the earth shook again, and the red stars jumped in tandem.

Dux said, "Do you remember where Aphrodite said her husband was? Hephaestus?"

"Yes, she said he was here, in the West. But what is the connection?"

"Hephaestus is a powerful being. He's best known as the god of metalworking, fire, forges, and sculpture."

"How powerful is he?"

"Very. He's revered as a god, and he's supposedly the son of Zeus. He and Aphrodite have a tumultuous marriage. I won't get into the sordid details, but I will say that you are not the first person with whom Aphrodite has flirted, and that you demonstrated far more restraint than most of her subjects. Unfortunately,

Hephaestus is motivated more by his emotions than his intellect. Rumors that you were flirting with Aphrodite, or that she placed her hand upon your chest, would make him furious. I fear that has happened."

Gaius was confused. "What has that got to do with the two pillars ahead, or the red stars?"

"What you see were not pillars, and those," said Dux, pointing at the red orbs ahead, "are not stars."

Before Gaius could ask his companion what he meant, something big slammed violently into the path just ahead of them. Gaius instinctively threw his arms in front of his face as his body was pelted by a shower of rocks, dirt, and vegetation.

"What was that?" he asked, wiping debris from his face.

"A tree fell," replied his guide, doing the same.

"A tree fell?"

"Yes – from the sky. Come here!" Dux took hold of his companion's arm and pulled him forward hastily. "We must use it to protect ourselves."

Gaius looked up. Only a few feet away was the bottom of a tree's root ball, which was as tall as he was. Smelly clumps of earth continued to fall from its spiderlike roots and bugs skittered away from the mass, some crawling up his legs, others over his feet.

"That should give you some idea how gigantic our opponent is," said Dux, when the two men were concealed. "He threw this tree like a lawn dart. Unfortunately, there are plenty more lawn darts to be had in this forest."

"Who is *he?*" asked Gaius.

"Talos."

"Who is Talos?"

"Talos is a sixty-foot tall, animate statue, or automaton. He – and I say 'he' because the statue resembles a male soldier in battle garb – is made of bronze, which makes him virtually indestructible. He was built by, and is commanded by, Hephaestus."

Gaius's shoulders drooped. "Then he is here to kill me for speaking to Aphrodite."

"That's a logical assumption. Talos has been trained to kill by throwing things at his prey, such as large rocks, trees, cattle, or even other people. Alternatively, he may simply squash you under a bronze heel."

"But you said the path we are on will shock any creature than intends to harm us."

"Talos isn't on the path, Gaius. He's straddling it. His legs are those things you took to be pillars. The red stars are his eyes."

"What can we do?"

Dux thought for a moment before replying, "Do you recall why everyone on the other side of the West Gate is paid by the Warden?"

"Yes – because he's a fair man who treats everyone equally."

"Right. Equality is important in the West. On the other side of the West Gate, the emphasis is on treating every man the same – whether high or low, rich or poor. Everyone is on the same level. On this side of the gate, it's just the opposite. Here, might makes right. The strong dominate the weak. Talos is strong, and we are, in a relative sense, quite weak."

"I agree," said Gaius, trembling. The earth was shaking as Talos approached, nearer and nearer. BOOM-BOOM-BOOM...

"But what can we do?" he asked again.

"The answer is obvious, is it not? We must restore equality by bringing him down to our level!"

"You have a plan?"

"I do."

A minute later, Gaius stood atop the tree that Talos had thrown and watched with trepidation as the muscled bronze monster moved closer, one screeching metallic step at a time. In the twilight, illuminated by the rising moon, Talos's sculpted body was a menacing black specter, its blazing, angry red eyes never moving from its prey. Gaius sensed that the thing harbored a personal animosity for him, the mortal who had "wronged" its master.

The giant was now less than twenty yards away.

"May I please run now?" Gaius pleaded.

"Not yet," came Dux's voice from nearby.

"How much longer?"

"I'll tell you when to run. Don't worry. Do you remember our discussion on the four cardinal virtues?"

Gaius blew out a breath. He was not in the mood for a lesson. Still, he replied, "Yes. Temperance, Fortitude, Prudence, and Justice!"

"Right. Your recall that in the beautiful wilderness of temptations, Temperance is the most useful virtue for a man. Can you guess, then, what virtue is most useful here, in the wilderness of the West, where strength and power are the weapons of choice?"

Gaius trembled as the giant grew closer. "Fortitude?"

"Exactly. Fortitude. That is the virtue that enables you to undergo pain, peril, or danger. Is that not appropriate, under the circumstances?"

The younger man just managed a nod. "Yes, but...well, shouldn't that be virtue be applied prudently? There are some dangers that merit running away, aren't there? Like a bronze giant with red eyes that can throw trees at you? I mean...well, I do not wish to appear to be a coward, but confronting Talos head-on seems a bit..." Gaius swallowed. "Rash?"

"Fortitude is the middle ground between rashness and cowardice. Be strong, Gaius. I won't fail you."

Talos, now illuminated by the light of the moon, moved closer, and closer, until he was a stone's throw from his target. There he stopped, crouched at the waist, and jutted his bronze, bearded chin forward. It was an aggressive – almost taunting – gesture. It conveyed, *"Here I am, mortal! What are you going to do about it?"*

Gaius stepped back and almost fell when his foot struck a small branch. He threw his arms out and just managed to maintain his balance.

He couldn't retreat much further. He was running out of tree.

Talos took a step closer, a huge bronze right foot landing near the fallen tree's branches. The branches were hardly an obstacle for the monster, however. He was massive and strong. He knew, in some primitive way, that when he moved forward, the tree would yield, and Gaius would fall, and then Hephaestus's honor would be restored.

Talos's left foot swung forward...

...then abruptly stopped, in mid-air. For the first time since the encounter began, the statue moved its eyes away from Gaius. It seemed to sense that something was wrong.

The creature swayed.

"Now!" yelled Dux from the nearby woods.

Gaius didn't move. He was hypnotized by the immensity of the thing that teetered above him. Though he couldn't see Talos's face, and though he knew it was sculpted bronze, and thus unchanged, Gaius imagined that the monster's formerly stoic expression was now one of confusion.

"Run," yelled Dux. "Run, or you'll be crushed!"

That registered. Gaius blinked and saw Talos's glowing eyes racing toward him in a downward arc. The animated statue was falling!

The young traveler jumped, and not a second too soon. He'd not even reached Dux's hiding place before Talos hit the ground, his face slamming into the earth exactly where Gaius had been standing. The impact was so terrible that it rocketed Gaius off his feet and into the air, his arms flailing. He hit the ground hard - but not as hard as Talos.

Moaning, the traveler rose to one knee. Looking back, he saw Dux already standing on the statue's right heel, prying something from Talos's left ankle with his staff. His grunts indicated he wasn't having much success.

"Don't just stand there!" he yelled. "Help me!"

Talos, still flat on the ground, lifted his elbows above his back and planted his massive hands on the ground, near his waist. The movement was slow but deliberate. Talos's metal skin stretched and groaned.

"Hurry!" yelled Dux. "He's trying to stand up!"

Gaius rushed to Dux's side. He saw that there was a huge bronze nail, or plug, in Talos's ankle, and that his guide was desperately trying to dislodge it. The younger man crouched over the bronze object, grasped it, and began pulling with all his strength.

The nail began to give, and a purplish liquid began to seep from the opening.

Talos shuddered and tried to pull his left foot forward, but the movement was stopped by the rope that Dux and Gaius had extended between two trees on either side of the path – the very rope that had tripped Talos and brought the monster down to their level.

"Talos!" yelled Dux, "Stay as you are!" He looked at Gaius. "Pull harder!"

Gaius did, leaning backward and grunting loudly, the muscles in his arms quivering.

The nail moved, then came free, and more liquid splashed from the ruptured heel. Gaius peered down and saw a pool of the purple stuff inside the hollow foot of the creature, and guessed that the living statue must be filled with it.

"Well done!" said Dux, grabbing his staff. He jumped to the ground. "Now, I'm going to have a discussion with our friend here."

"Discussion?" yelled Gaius, looking up. "He can talk?"

"No," said Dux, moving. "But he can hear."

The guide strode forward quickly, saying, "Talos! Stay where you are! If you rise, you will bleed to death!"

The statue froze, except for its head, which turned toward Dux, its neck making the now-familiar sound of metal being twisted. Its red eyes were a little less bright than they had been. Its expression was as impassive as ever.

Dux moved until he was standing before the titan's nose. The head of the automaton was almost as wide as the guide was tall. Dux turned to look it in the eyes – one of them, anyway.

"Listen," he said. "I know you think you are doing the right thing, but my friend is innocent of the charges made by your master. You know of my Order, and you know that I would not defend a guilty man. I do not wish to harm you, but neither do I want you to harm my friend. We've removed the plug from your heel. So long as you remain where you are, you will live, but if you stand, the liquid that sustains you will pour from your heel, and you will die. Do you understand?"

Talos did not respond, but neither did he attempt to move.

"I will send for Hephaestus. He will find and repair you, so that you may continue your role as his servant. You need only wait here, as you are, and stay very still. That should be easy for you since you are, after all, a statue."

Dux looked back and saw Gaius dropping the bronze nail to the ground. Knowing that Talos could not see this, he said, "We have hidden the plug in the forest. If you stand, you will bleed out before you find it. Your vision is already impaired by the slight blood loss you've experienced. You know what will happen to you if lose consciousness. You are made of the finest bronze in the world. The beings of this realm will fall upon you like ants on a pile of sugar and disassemble you."

He touched Talos's massive cheek and said, "Truly, we mean you no harm, and have done no wrong. I hope you will not hold this against us. We seek only to live another day. The same as you."

With that, he lowered his hand from the creature's metallic flesh and moved back to Gaius.

"Let's move," he said.

"Shouldn't we hide the nail?"

"Of course not. What if Talos ignores my advice and stands up? I don't want to kill the dumb beast. If he stands, he'll still be weakened by the blood he'll lose while searching for the nail. He will find it, of course, and he'll be able to reinsert it and save his life, but at that point, he'll be too weak to pursue us. We need only put some distance between him and ourselves before that happens. Remember, too, that should we truly harm Talos, or intend to, we would violate the rules of the straight and narrow path. It would shock us and force us into the dark forest. Do you want to walk among the trees, where all sorts of wicked creatures and men might find us?"

"No."

"Good. Let's be on our way then!"

CHAPTER 9

THE REALM OF DARKNESS

ours passed. There was no discernible boundary line between the Western Wilderness and the North, yet Gaius instinctively realized they had arrived in the North when the last rays of the sun vanished beneath the horizon.

Gaius had never imagined there could exist so dark, cold, and dreary place as the northern realm. The only light – and it was more a weakening of the darkness, than light – came from the spectral clouds that circled above, which were inexplicably, and feebly, fluorescent. Because of this, the North was not black, but instead the very darkest shade of gray.

The terrain was rugged and rocky, with sparse, sickly vegetation consisting mostly of thorny bushes without leaves or flowers. Merely walking was difficult because of the seemingly infinite number of hidden, fist-sized rocks that twisted the travelers' ankles every other step, causing them to constantly stumble.

The wind howled relentlessly, sometimes roaring so loudly that the two men were unable to communicate even when yelling. At other times, the wind sounded more like the moan of a dying animal – sorrowful, scared, and pleading.

"I do not like this place," said Gaius during one of the wind's respites. "Surely no one lives in such a horrible and desolate land as this."

"You're wrong," responded his guide. "There are people all around us, working and living in tiny villages that dot the great and otherwise barren plains. There is a legend that says there was once a thriving community in the North, long, long ago. It is said the people here once built a great tower that reached almost to the heavens."

Gaius was dubious. "Then where is this tower?"

"It collapsed, supposedly."

"Do you think it really existed?"

Dux shrugged. "I can't prove it. No man can. But I have spent years looking for the ruins, and here and there I have found giant blocks that I believe were once part of the doomed edifice. I suspect that the ruins are lost because all the blocks have been salvaged and transported to the far corners of the world to be incorporated into newer buildings."

Gaius considered this. "Then you might yet find clues as to how the tower was constructed, and what it looked like, by a systematic study of the pieces that are now spread around the world."

"If I can find them, yes, and properly apply the rules of Geometry and other sciences to deduce their origins. There's much work to be done in that regard."

Gaius spotted the hint. Clearly, his companion savored the thought of traveling the world in search of lost things, and perhaps deducing their natures and origins. And Gaius suddenly realized that he, himself, was such a man, and that he had finally found someone who shared his passions. He said nothing, but the recognition warmed his heart.

The travelers arrived at the jagged crest of a large hill. Looking down, Gaius could see a marsh below, and beyond that, a body of water, on the shore of which was a large bonfire that illuminated the immediate area. There was a spectral, undulating mist that made it impossible for him to ascertain whether the body of water was a river, lake, or sea. But he could make out a dilapidated ferry on the nearest shore, and next to it, a menacing figure in a black robe. The figure was facing inland.

"That's the ferryman of the North," said Dux. "This is where he waits for passengers."

"Where does he ferry them to?" asked Gaius.

"An undiscovered country."

"Are we–"

"No. Not today, anyway." He pointed. "But look there! Prospective passengers."

Gaius saw that his guide was pointing at a trail that was illuminated by torches attached to iron posts. Three emaciated men shuffled along the path toward the river. Their thin, ashen flesh was stretched tightly over their bones and their simple clothing – tunics and pants – were in tatters. Their hair was unkempt and matted with mud and vegetation, and their feet were bare and bloodied.

"Liches," whispered Dux. "The walking dead."

Gaius saw this must be true. The foul creature at the head of the group had his arms wrapped tightly around his stomach, as if he were trying to keep his intestines from falling out of his body. Bizarrely, smoke bellowed from his midsection, and the stench of burning flesh soon reached Gaius's nose, making him nauseous.

The pathetic creature was looking over his shoulder and yelling, "Hurry! Hurry! There is a boat ahead! It will carry us away! We can make our escape!"

The second man seemed not to notice the other's plea. He had his arms stretched high above him. He was trying to capture a bird that flew just above his head but outside of his grasp. It carried something in its talons that the man clearly wanted, though Gaius was unable to make out what it could be. Whatever it was, it was dripping something onto the man's upturned face. The man jumped into the air, again and again, trying to grasp the object, but in vain. Each time he jumped, the bird rose.

Gaius could hear the man crying, "Give it back! Give it back!"

The third man seemed oblivious to both of his companions. He trudged silently forward with his head lowered. His chin and neck were crimson and wet and his head bobbled in all directions in a strange manner.

"What sad, pitiful wretches they are," said Dux, shaking his head slowly.

"I wonder what they could have done to deserve this fate?"

"Something truly terrible, I imagine. But the ferryman below is not who they think he is, and there is no escape from that sad shore. Let's keep moving."

The two men descended the hill to the path they had spied below, though far behind the sad troupe they had spied earlier. Because the path was illuminated by torches, Dux tapped his staff into the ground three times, extinguishing the magical light.

"No reason to attract attention," he said.

"Are we nearing the North Gate?" asked Gaius.

"No, my friend. There is no North Gate. There is only a dilapidated wall and the ruins of what might have once been a gate, and a pillar, long ago, when Thuban reigned."

"Then what is the Warden's function here?"

"There is no Warden in the North."

Gaius was surprised and disheartened. "Why not?"

"The Master's authority does not extend into this realm."

"Can we stop at the ruins, at least, and rest?"

"No, the North is too dangerous. Our knights never stop in the North, and neither shall we."

As the two trudged forward, Gaius said, "If the South is the land of beauty, and the West is the land of strength, what characteristic exemplifies the North?"

Dux didn't hesitate. "Ignorance."

Surprised, Gaius said, "I cannot imagine how ignorance can ever be a good thing, unlike beauty and strength, which you have shown may be either good or bad, depending on how they are used. Is there something that separates one region of the North from the other, in the way that the southern and western realms are separated into civilized and wild, or tame and untamed, regions? Is there a civilized ignorance and an untamed ignorance?"

"Yes. The people who live in this part of the realm live in darkness because they have mistaken darkness for light. They believe this darkness is all there is. Yet there is hope that a few of them might still be saved."

Dux pointed at the inky blackness in the far distance, which had the appearance of a great storm consisting of the darkest imaginable clouds. "But there is no hope in the land ahead of us, which is the Northern Wilderness. The inhabitants there are aware of light, yet despise it. They are born of darkness and turn to ash if the least ray of light touches their flesh. Chaos, anarchy, and destruction are objects of worship there. Ignorance is bliss, and bliss is death."

At this point, the travelers had reached the end of the lighted path. Here, several large sections of fallen pillars littered the ground. The sections were sculpted from black stone. Some sections remained upright while others lay on their sides.

"Does this place have a name?" Gaius asked.

"It did, but that has been lost to time. Today, there are some who call it 'Hiram's Lament,' and others, 'Hiram's Folly,' but I cannot tell you why."

Gaius spotted what he thought had once been the base of the pillar, and could just make out an inscription at the bottom: *Erebus.* He also saw stairs descending to what he thought might be a crypt, and he wondered who would be buried in such a forsaken place. He thought it must be someone very important, since the door of the underground chamber appeared to be made of gold.

All around the travelers, and for as far as Gaius could see, were mounds of stone rubble as tall and wide as a house. There was just enough room between them for two men to walk abreast.

"This is like a maze," observed Gaius.

"Yes, and a very extensive one."

"Do you know of a path that will lead us to the other side?"

Dux shook his head. "No. The landscape changes each time I come here."

"Why should that happen?"

"Because this is the home of a creature who feasts on the ignorant. He delights in confounding travelers. He moves the rubble constantly so that the path from one side to the other is never the same. We call him Solomon's Pet."

"Why do you call him that?"

"Because, like King Solomon, he loves riddles."

Before Gaius could reply, a strange creature emerged from behind one of the mounds and walked leisurely toward an intersection in front of the men. It was as big as an elephant, but had the form of a lion, except that it boasted large wings and, most remarkably, a human head. Atop its head and extending to its shoulders was a hood that seemed to be made of scale mail. Its lips were as black as coal, as were its pointed eyebrows and pupils.

Lowering its belly to the ground and extending its front paws in front of it, the creature smiled and said to Dux, "You called, traveler?"

The thing's voice was almost a growl, and Gaius observed that though the head was human, the teeth within the mouth were feline - as were the creature's terrifyingly oversized claws.

When Gaius found his breath, he said, "A sphinx? Is that a sphinx?"

"Yes," said Dux, taking a step forward.

The sphinx smiled an unfriendly smile. "You seek a path through my maze?"

"We do," answered Dux.

The smile grew wider. "Prove yourself and I will give you the route."

"I am well aware of your rules," replied Dux. He turned to Gaius. "The sphinx will challenge us with three riddles. If we provide the correct answers, he will tell us how to escape his maze. If we give the wrong answers...." Dux scratched behind one ear and gave his companion an apologetic look. "Well, it's best not to give the wrong answers."

Gaius blanched. "But why three questions? Shouldn't one suffice?"

Dux shook his head. "No. Everything here is done in threes."

The sphinx sneered. "You've made the boy a charity case. You throw answers at his questions without discretion. Have you forgotten the lessons my ancestors taught your Order? Are you unable to remain silent? Can you not keep secrets? Have you thrown aside the veil to usher in the public?"

The guide pivoted to face the creature. "No need to be unpleasant. We have not forgotten the lessons of your ancestors. But we do not, like you, treat trivial information as currency. Pose your riddles to me, not my friend. If a price is to be paid for a wrong answer, I, alone, will pay it."

The sphinx looked displeased. "But you will share your reward with him if you solve the riddles correctly. You will show him how to escape my maze."

"If I earn a reward, it is mine, and I will do with it as I please."

The sphinx shifted its black eyes to one side, saying, "Then you must whisper your answers to my riddles to me alone, and swear that, should they be correct, you will not share them with your companion." The creature licked its lips and returned its eyes to Dux. "Those are my terms."

Dux turned, saying to Gaius, "Should this go badly, and I can no longer serve as your guide, I suggest you wait here for another knight of the Order to pass through."

"I would rather it not go badly."

"We are of one mind," sighed Dux, moving forward until he was mere inches from the sphinx's face. "Ask me your riddles. I will take the three at once, since some may be easier to answer than others, and may afford me a few more seconds of life."

The creature again licked its lips and said, "Very well," and posed the following riddles:

1.   What traveler cannot be seen in darkness, even when illuminated by the sun?

2.   Though I remain whole, with nothing added or subtracted, when put to work, I will weigh less, more, and the same. What am I?

3.   What is a high hill and a low vale, when not a hill and a low vale?

CHAPTER 10

THE NORTHERN WILDERNESS

An hour later, a still mercifully intact Dux led Gaius out of the maze and into the untamed North.

"Now comes the hard part," said Dux.

"I thought nearly being eaten by a sphinx was the hard part."

"No, 'nearly' isn't hard at all. But never mind that. We are now entering the Northern Wilderness. In the heart of this forsaken land is a spinning black ocean that sucks in all light and extinguishes it. Its immensity is unfathomable. For the uninitiated, the merest glimpse of its waters, or the horrible creatures that float above them, causes madness. For that reason, you must be blindfolded."

"Why must I be blindfolded? Can't I just keep my eyes shut?"

"No. There are creatures in the wilderness who will approach you and try to convince you to open them. They can be quite persuasive."

"Won't you intervene?"

"I won't be able to. Most of the creatures do not have a physical form. They will speak to you directly, inside your head, and I will not hear them. When that happens, you must ignore them. Do not answer their questions. Do not comment on their statements. Do not bargain with them. Do not ponder their promises. And most importantly, never trust them. They are all liars, and they are masters of deception."

He stopped walking and turned toward his charge. "Don't listen to *me*, either."

"Why not?"

"The beings can imitate any voice, and they will speak to you, using mine, to try to get you to do things. But I will *not* speak to you until we reach the safety of a place known as the Northeast Corner. If you hear my voice before then, it is a trick. They might make you think that I am angry with you, or they may create the illusion that I am injured or abducted and pleading for help. Ignore all of that."

"But how shall we communicate, if you cannot speak to me?"

"We'll communicate manually, through certain grips that I'm going to teach you. It will be like hand signals, but done by touch. They are useful in places of darkness. Here," Dux said, removing a length of rope that had been innocuously wrapped several times about his waist. Gaius had thought the rope was a belt.

"Tie one end of this around your waist and I'll use the other end to lead you to the Northeast Corner."

Gaius took the rope and complied, saying, "You won't be very far away, will you? How long is this rope?"

"Don't worry. I will endeavor to stay close by, but so long as you are at one end and I am at the other, I will come to your aid should anything befall you."

"What happens if we are attacked – physically, I mean?"

"That's my problem," replied Dux.

"But...well, shouldn't I have a weapon of some kind, just in case?"

Dux chuckled. "No, because using it would require you to remove your blindfold and open your eyes, which is something you do *not* want to do. I value my life, and I don't want you swinging a weapon about while blindfolded."

Gaius frowned. He didn't like the idea of venturing into such a dangerous place blind and unarmed.

Dux squinted at him. "You don't have a weapon, do you?"

"No."

"Have you picked anything up that could be *used* as a weapon?"

"Like what?"

"Something of a metallic nature, for example?"

"No. I have nothing but my fists."

His guide grabbed the free end of the rope and wrapped it around his left forearm. "Good. Keep those in reserve. Now, take my hand and we will go over the signals."

Gaius complied, and his guide taught him some basic grips.

That done, Dux said, "As you can see, we will have to maneuver over some rubble to get to the other side. I'm going to blindfold you now, and then I'm going to take you by the arm and lead you forward as far as possible. There will be areas where we will be separated and have to rely on the rope, instead. It's going to be a little scary."

It took a long time to navigate through the rows of rubble. The two men locked arms and inched forward slowly, Dux steering Gaius through the obstacle course via a series of gentle tugs and pushes. Despite this, Gaius stubbed a toe on three different occasions.

"Well," said Dux, "this is more difficult than I expected. I think that, for now, we should remove your blindfold and let you walk on your own. We'll put it back on at the first sign of trouble."

Gaius was more than a little confused. Still blind, he said, "Then why was it necessary for me to keep my eyes closed while we-"

He felt his guide squeeze his hand and a grip that meant, "Stop."

This was followed by another signal: "Danger."

Reality slapped Gaius in the face. He broke into a cold sweat.

Dux hadn't spoken to him.

Something else had.

Scared and humiliated by just how easily he'd been duped, he returned Dux's sign with his own: "Yes." He didn't have a sign for "I understand," but hoped this sufficed.

Dux squeezed his hand twice, which Gaius knew was intended to reassure him. But the clever attack had rattled the young man. What if he'd simply done what the voice had told him to do? Would he now be dead, or *merely* insane?

The men continued to move forward, side by side, their arms intertwined.

"Hello, Gaius."

The words appeared in Gaius's head without warning. It was a woman's voice, and the tone was casual – almost playful.

Gaius clenched his teeth and squeezed his lips together.

"Cat got your tongue?" asked the voice. It/she laughed, but it was a friendly laugh. "I understand. *Don't speak to the ghosts*, right? But I'm no ghost. I'm the voice of reason."

Gaius remained silent.

"Look," said the voice. "I realize that you have put your trust in the man beside you, and his Order. But why? In hopes of gaining 'secrets?' Gaius, *they have no secrets!* None worth having, anyway. But you'll only learn that after swearing an oath of loyalty to them. How can you be so gullible?"

Gaius felt a spectral hand brush his cheek. "If it's secrets you want, stop now and come with me. Why follow the frail being beside you, who in his wildest dreams can only *hope* to learn what I *already* know. *I* can teach you magic. *I* can show you the future. *I* can teach you how to turn lead into gold."

The voice snickered. "The Order lost its way a long time ago, Gaius. It had magic once, and power, and prestige, but now it is nothing but a bunch of old men who use fools like you to cut wood for them. You suspect that, in your heart, don't you?"

A second passed. "Ah, yes...I can feel your doubt. Just remove your blindfold, Gaius, and I will rescue you from the shyster who is leading your astray."

Gaius ignored the voice, focusing instead on the movement of his feet. Left, right, left, right...

"Sister, leave him be," came a second voice - this one, male. "Gaius is not the man you think he is. He's not after secrets, or prestige, or magic, or fortune. He's not as petty as that. Gaius seeks only one thing: truth. Yes, truth! That is why he is traveling East. He knows that his reality is a dream and he wants to wake from it and see the world as it truly is. Isn't that right, Gaius?"

Gaius ground his teeth. Right, left, right, left...

"Then again," said the voice, "what *is* truth? I'm sorry, Gaius, but you are chasing an illusion. There is no such thing. There is no path that will lead you to it. What you see is what you get. Brutality, war, anger, greed, jealousy...there's your truth. You're an animal and you and your kind behave as animals. There is no 'higher level.' Even the thing that you think makes your species unique – consciousness – is just a flickering fire in that gray, soft brain of yours."

Right, left, right...

"If you earnestly seek truth, why do you hide your eyes? Hasn't your guide told you of the wonders that are, at this moment, all around you? True, many people find them frightening. Yet they are real and, in their way, magnificent. Will the sight of them drive you insane? What does it matter? Insanity is simply a readjustment of the psyche that permits a normal man to comprehend extraordinary things. You cannot simultaneously seek truth and hide from it. *Open your eyes, Gaius, and see!*"

Gaius felt sand blowing across his feet. The ground was growing softer and each step became more laborious than the next. He heard something roaring in the distance, to his left. It sounded like the winds of a mighty storm, but there was an underlying sound, too. Moans? Cries for help? Screams?

The air got colder. The traveler trembled, and at that moment, the ground under his feet gave way. He fell hard on his right side and immediately began sliding north, feet first, as if the ground was sloped and covered in ice. Confused, Gaius threw out his hands and frantically grasped for anything that he could use to stop his slide, but the only thing his hands found was sand.

Gaius's terror grew as he realized that he wasn't sliding.

The sands were *carrying* him.

To *their* master.

He took in a breath to scream, but before he could, the rope around his body tightened and his slide came to an abrupt halt. Gaius heard Dux grunt loudly. For a moment, the traveler had hope, but then he felt himself again sliding north, and he assumed with utter despair that his companion had dropped the other end of the rope.

Then, the rope again became taut, and his slide was again stopped. A second later, he felt himself being pulled backward, against the flow of the sand, and he realized that his guide had not lost his hold. The guide had been pulled off his feet, perhaps, but he'd maintained a steadfast grip on the lifeline between himself and the young traveler he was responsible for.

"Untie yourself!" came a voice. "You guide can't keep this up! The sands are stronger than he is. He's about to fall and then he will be sucked into the abyss with you! Do you want to be responsible for his death? Are you so selfish?"

As if to confirm the voice's words, Gaius felt himself slipping back toward the impetuous sea of nothingness. His guide was fighting the fast-moving sands but losing.

"Save him!" whispered the voice. "Untie yourself!"

Still blind, Gaius searched for the knot that held the rope around his waist in place.

Again, he jerked to a stop. Again, he felt his guide pulling him back from the brink, but this time with more urgency. Gaius tried to help by kicking his heels into the sand, but there was nothing to push against. Realizing that his thrashing was probably hindering his companion's efforts, he stopped and let his body go limp.

The return from the brink of the abyss was slow but steady. When, at last, his body came to rest, he felt Dux pulling him upright. The sands became still.

The two men struggled to their feet and, side-by-side, began walking again. There was no rest in the Northern Wilderness.

CHAPTER 11

THE NORTHEAST CORNER

The two men traveled for a long time in silence. Gaius never imagined that remaining silent could be such a trial, but it was, and doubly so because he was walking blind in a cold and hostile land. He had a million questions for his guide but more than anything wanted to hear a real person's voice. The phantoms that whispered in his ears incessantly were ingenious and persuasive in their attempts to get Gaius to remove his blindfold and open his eyes. He had so far resisted, but he was growing weaker by the minute. His legs were sore, his body was bruised, his throat was dry, and his mind was increasingly foggy.

It was in this weary state that he felt calloused fingers creeping beneath his blindfold. Alarmed, he reached up in an attempt to ward them off, but it was too late. The blindfold was gone.

"No worries, my friend."

It was his guide's voice.

Or was it?

Gaius held out his hand, licked his parched lips, and mumbled, "Is that you, Dux?"

He felt his guide taking his hand, and then the signal: *Yes*.

"You can open your eyes now," the other man said. "We've reached the Northeast Corner, which marks the boundary line between the North and East. We're safe."

Not quite believing what he was told, Gaius blinked once, very quickly. A weak light caressed his eyes. He waited for a second, and when he didn't die, he blinked again, and again he didn't die.

Taking a deep breath, he opened his eyes and kept them open. There was light. It was a very dim light, coming from somewhere very far away, but it was real.

"Take a minute," said his guide from behind him, clapping him on the shoulder. "Give yourself time to adjust. I'll untie the rope."

Gaius nodded and slowly surveyed his surroundings. The land was in shadow, the only light being the first pink rays of the still-hidden sun in the East. The land was flat and the vegetation sparse. There were many boulders, some the size of a horse, and some of which were stacked atop one another. Between them were waist-high grasses that danced lazily in the chilly morning breeze. It was a land in transition. Not as barren as the North, but not as alive as the South.

The most remarkable feature was the object directly ahead of him: a giant stone that had been crudely hewn into a block that was perhaps five feet in height, half as thick, and nearly twice as wide. A mallet and chisel rested on a nearby slab.

"What is that?" he asked as his guide struggled with the knotted rope.

Dux didn't lift his head. "That, my friend, is the *Rough Ashlar*. It's a waypoint, or marker, for travelers. It tells them they've reached the Northeast Corner. As you can see, there's no great pillar here and no gate. Just that stone."

"Who made it?"

"Nature made it, of course. With regard to who shaped it into its current form, however, that is the work of many men. Tens of thousands, at least. When our Order was established, and we began traveling this path on a regular basis, it became the custom for each traveler to make a single cut into the stone. A *single* cut, mind you. No more, no less. Our aim is to someday make this stone into a perfect ashlar."

"What do you mean by *perfect?*"

"Every edge square and sharp, the horizontal aspects perfectly level, and vertical aspects perfectly perpendicular."

"You wish to accomplish that with each traveler making but a single cut?"

"A single cut each time he passes, yes. He might make several over the course of his life if he travels frequently."

Gaius shook his head. "Unless there are a great many travelers, I do not think you will accomplish your objective."

"You may be right. We've been at it for a very, very long time, and there are fewer travelers today than there used to be. But it is our custom, and we take some satisfaction in knowing that each strike brings us closer to our goal."

"Why is it called an *ashlar?* Why not just call it a stone or a block?"

"Well..." mumbled Dux, pausing to think. "Consider that one of the most perfectly cut stones in the world is a diamond. Do you know what a diamond is made of?"

"No," admitted Gaius.

"Carbon. Guess where carbon is readily found."

Gaius hadn't any idea what carbon was, so he remained silent.

Dux gave him the answer. "Ash. If you squeeze enough ash together, using tremendous pressure, the substance will become a diamond. You might say that by turning this stone into a perfect block, we hope to turn ash into a diamond. Do you understand?"

Gaius thought about this. "So..." he ventured, "this stone is made of ash?"

"No, Gaius. I'm speaking *metaphorically*. I am giving you a way to easily remember both the name of the stone – ashlar - and its role in our rituals. To us, metaphorically, a rough ashlar is a *diamond in the rough*. We hope to perfect it and make it a *perfect* ashlar. Do you understand?"

Gaius nodded, though he wasn't completely satisfied. He would now remember the stone's name – ashlar – but still had no idea why it was called that. He wondered if even his guide knew.

He said, "Will I be allowed to strike the stone before we continue east?"

"No. You've had no training and wouldn't know where to make the next cut. But if all goes well, you'll have many opportunities to improve upon the ashlar in the future. For now, we must focus on our trip to the East. It is unfortunate that you've lost a shoe."

"What?" asked Gaius, surprised. He looked down and saw that his guide was correct. The ground had been so soft and sandy that Gaius hadn't even noticed the loss. "It must have flown off when I was fighting against the sands."

"Well, don't worry. I'm sure another traveler will find it and return it to you." Dux grunted. "I did a fine job with this knot. You're bleeding, too. See there? Your knee. It's just an abrasion. The sand in the North is sharp, like powdered glass." Dux handed the ends of the still tied rope to Gaius, saying, "Here, you work on the knot and I'll tend to your wound."

Dux knelt and rolled up the tattered pants leg until it was folded neatly above Gaius's wounded knee, then applied a blindfold as a bandage over the wound.

As he stood, Gaius said, "I think the knot tightened when I was being pulled. I can't undo it. It's as if the fibers of the rope have bound themselves to one another."

"I thought the same. Unfortunately, neither of us has a blade. For now, just wrap the rope around your body. When we get to the East, we'll have someone remove it."

"Very well," replied Gaius, following his guide's instructions.

As he did so, Dux said, "What do you think of my home?"

"Your home? You *live* here?"

"Yes. My cottage is very near."

Gaius looked around him. "It seems...well, it seems an odd place to build a cottage. Does it not bother you that you are so close to the northern darkness?"

"Not at all. Have you not heard that it is always darkest before the dawn? My home faces the East, not the North. I look forward, not backward."

"But why did you choose to build a home here, instead of the East? Or the South, or the West?"

"It wasn't my decision. I am only here temporarily, in a rotational capacity. Eventually, another member of our Order will replace me, and when his time is up, he'll be replaced. The small cottage that we occupy during our tenure was constructed by the Order long ago. It's essentially an outpost. We use it to welcome travelers and guests, and to ensure they reach the East safely."

"That must keep you busy. How long have you been stationed here?"

Dux held up a finger. "Not *stationed*, my friend. I was *placed* here."

"What's the difference?"

"Think about it. What does *stationary* mean?"

Gaius shrugged. "In one place, or..." He thought a moment longer. "Unmoving?"

"Just so. But as you are aware, I've been busy escorting you from realm to realm. If this was my *station* – a place I could not move from - I'd be derelict in my duties, wouldn't I? The only members of our Order who are *stationed* are the Wardens. Can you guess why?"

Gaius thought for a moment, then ventured, "Because they guard the gates?"

"Exactly. The gates must *always* be guarded, which means the men who guard the gates must remain near them *at all times*. Thus, only the Wardens of the East, West, and South have a *station*. The other officers have only a *place* because their duties require them to be mobile. You may think this unimportant, but trust me, it is not."

"As you say," agreed Gaius. "Do you like your *place*?"

"Yes. I enjoy meeting young men like you who wish to join us. But, in truth, I'm worried about the future of this outpost. I sense that the darkness of the North is advancing. I think we're losing ground here, and that someday, we may be forced to retreat."

"What does that mean?" asked Gaius.

"It means that there would be no more travelers, my friend. Eventually, there might be no one left to guard the gates. Then the darkness of the North will expand, and all the evils it conceals."

Seeing the effect of his words on his companion, Dux waved away the gloomy picture he'd painted. "What do I know, though? Things ebb and flow. Perhaps tomorrow the darkness will retreat. I'm a guide, not a prophet."

He retrieved his staff and smiled. "Let's go."

CHAPTER 12

THE REALM OF WISDOM

The boulder-littered ground of the northeast gave way to the grassy fields of the East. Trees became more numerous and varied in type, and ponds began to dot the landscape. The weary travelers began to move through a low vale surrounded by many high hills. The rising sun peeked between two of those hills, bathing the world in a golden light. The air was fresh, crisp, and invigorating.

After reaching the crest of one hill, Gaius spotted a village in the distance. The buildings there resembled the letter A, the walls angled upward until they intersected, negating the need for a roof. They were situated due east and West, with the sun rising above them. On a very high hill, perhaps a mile behind the village, was the titanic pillar that Gaius had expected.

Seeing the traveler's eyes light up, Dux said, "Yes, there it is. The pillar that marks the location of the Eastern Gate - the Pillar of Wisdom."

"Is that that the pursuit of the citizens here? Wisdom?"

"The pursuit, and the practice. This is the land of wysards."

This caused Gaius to stop in his tracks. He looked at his guide, eyes wide. "The people here are *wizards?*"

"That's right."

"You mean the people here practice magic?"

Dux shrugged. "Science and magic are often confused, my friend, and science is very important in this realm. Some outsiders believe that the Warden of the East is a great wysard, but that's because they lack an understanding of how the universe works. No, I call the people here wizards because that's what they are. The term 'wizard' is derived from an older term, 'wysard.' *Wise* was previously spelled as *w-y-s-e*. Wysard, or wizard, simply means 'wise one.' There are *wizards* in the East just as there are *dullards* in the North ."

Gaius was suspicious. "Is this another of your teaching tricks?"

His guide held up both hands to proclaim his innocence. "On my honor, it is not. A wizard is simply a wise person. The magic element was introduced later by the creative minds of our friends in the South. I believe confusion over the term is why some people believe that King Solomon practices magic. He's a very wise man, so, thanks to the novel interpretation of the term 'wizard,' many people assume he's a sorcerer. To avoid confusion in our realms, we prefer the 's' spelling of the word instead of the 'z.'"

Gaius pondered this. "Is King Solomon a citizen of the East?"

"He is an honorary member, as are other wise kings. Most kings *are not* wise, of course. There are many more kings in the West than there are in the East. This realm is primarily populated by philosophers, alchemists, scientists, mathematicians, engineers, and other cerebral sorts."

"I wonder that you say 'cerebral,' since a wise man is not necessarily an intelligent one, or vice versa. I do not think of wisdom and intelligence as the same thing."

Dux smiled at his companion. "An astute observation, my friend. I agree. They are not the same. Intelligence is a tool and wisdom is the proper application of that tool. But they are closely related and most potent when paired with one another. They are characteristics of the same kind of man – the kind most valued by our Order."

"Which is?"

"The *thinking* man." Dux motioned at the houses they were approaching. "If you could glimpse inside these homes, you'd find bookshelves, laboratories, blueprints, abacuses, telescopes, and all the other wonderful tools used to uncover the secrets of our reality."

"Do the citizens of the South and West not envy those in the East? With such great wisdom, the people here can achieve almost anything. Would the world not be a better place if all the realms were realms of wisdom? The occupations of the men in the South and West seem almost trivial in comparison."

"You're wrong, Gaius. Though we generally hold wisdom in higher esteem than strength or beauty, without the latter, the people of the East could accomplish very little. King Solomon contrived the great temple that is underway, but without the workers and the financing of the West, it would never be built, and without the artisans of the South, it might be an ugly monstrosity.

"In the same vein, a wise philosopher's thoughts will be lost if they are presented in a brutish and inarticulate manner. They must be presented in a way that is pleasing and beautiful. Beauty, strength, and wisdom are heart, muscle, and brain, and all are required for great and important undertakings."

The two walked for another minute in silence before Gaius said, "Why are there so few people about? It is morning. Shouldn't the citizens be working?"

"They are. But remember, this is the realm of wysards. They do most of their work indoors, where their books, laboratories, and other devices are. They are, in general, predisposed to a solitary lifestyle."

"Is it not too dark in their houses to work? The windows seem quite small."

"The people here use lamps, Gaius. That is why the oil burned in the lamps is so valuable to them. Thus, while the people in the South are paid in wine, as befits their occupation, and the people in the West are paid in corn, as befits theirs, the people in the East are paid in oil, so that their lamps may radiate a perpetual light."

"And what of that great building there?" the other traveler asked, pointing at a massive square structure that rose above the other buildings.

"That is the great library of the East," answered his guide. "It holds thousands of clay tablets from the Known and Unknown worlds dating back to the dawn of civilization - and a few even older than that. The tablets contain the secrets of sciences you cannot yet fathom."

"Why were the tablets made of clay?"

"Because at one time, clay was all we had to work with. There was no parchment or vellum in ancient times. But clay could be easily formed into square tablets, and symbols or runes pressed into the wet clay. When the clay dried, the tablets would be like bricks which would last almost forever. For that reason, clay has constantly been employed by people around the world to record important histories and findings. A good thing, too, since no scrolls of vellum or parchment would have endured what those tablets have endured. Because of their value, they are zealously guarded."

"Might we visit the library?"

"You know the answer, Gaius. We don't have time. In any event, you are not yet a member of our Order, and so are not qualified to see the tablets. You may do so later if things go well."

The men continued to walk until the village and its fabulous library was far behind them, and from there began ascending a hill via a number of stone steps. Gaius was ready when the BOOM of a nearby cannon blast assaulted his ears.

"We are near the East Gate," he said confidently.

"We are," confirmed his guide.

At the top of the hill was another corridor of statues. Gaius recognized only a few: Isis, Thoth, Odin, Athena, and Providentia on the left side of the path, and on the right, Socrates, Plato, Pythagoras, and Zeno. But there were many more, and Gaius promised himself that someday he would return to the East and learn the identities of all the wise heroes depicted.

Ahead of the men, though some distance away, was the silhouette of the titanic Pillar of Wisdom, and behind it, the dome of the rising sun.

Dux said, "Do you recall the architectural order of the Pillar of Beauty?"

"I recall it had leaves and what looked like a potted plant at the top," said Gaius. He thought a moment. "It was modeled after a woman carrying a basket on her head."

"That's right. A *thin* woman. Her name?"

"Corinthia - but not really. That was a trick to help me remember the type of pillar. *Corinthian.*"

"Very good. And what did the Pillar of Strength look like?"

"It was thicker and sturdier...and simpler. Not as beautiful, but strong. It had a square disc laid atop a round one at the top. It was called..." He frowned.

Dux said, "Was it strong enough to batter down a large door?"

Gaius snapped his fingers. "That's right. *Door.* Door...ick, right? *Doric.*"

His guide nodded. "If the Pillar of Beauty was beautiful, and the Pillar of Strength was strong, how do you imagine the Pillar of Wisdom will appear when we are closer to it?"

Gaius gazed at the distant column. "I cannot imagine how a pillar can be made to look *wise.*"

"Think harder, my friend. Scrolls are often used to record important information, yes?"

"Yes."

"Then it would be reasonable to use a scroll to symbolize wisdom. Do you agree?"

Gaius nodded. "Yes. Are you saying that the pillar is shaped like a scroll?"

"The capital is, yes. If you use your imagination. You'll see."

And soon enough, Gaius did see. As they moved closer and the Pillar of Wisdom came into view, the young traveler saw that it was not as narrow at the Pillar of Beauty, nor as thick as the Pillar of Strength, but the same height as both. At the top was a feature that looked exactly like a partially opened scroll, face down, the still curled portions hanging over the edges. The curled portions – left and right – resembled spirals.

"This pillar," said Dux, "is from the Ionic order."

Gaius said, "*Ionic*...it is an odd term. You have a technique to help me remember it?"

"Of course. To read a scroll, you must first lay your eyes on it. *Eyes on it*...Ionic. Simple enough. Or, you might see the spirals on either side of the pillar as eyes, in which case you can say that the pillar *has* eyes on it. The same thing approached differently."

"A scroll...*eyes on it*...yes, I think that will be easy to remember."

"Later, when you learn more about geometry, you might notice that the forms on either side of the pillar, which resemble the curled portions of an opened scroll, are reminiscent of what we call the 'golden spiral,' which occurs throughout nature. It's a scientific concept and should further reinforce your connection of this particular pillar to the concept of *wisdom*."

"As you say," agreed Gaius, but he was already distracted by his study of the many strange symbols that were carved into the base of the pillar. He could not imagine what they might mean, but knew better than to ask. If his guide had wished to share that knowledge, he would have.

The travelers next approached the East wall. It was as high as the walls in the South and West, but its blocks were not made of marble, as in the South, or granite, as in the West. Instead, the blocks were made of crystal so pure that they were almost transparent. Gaius wondered where the people of the East could quarry crystals of the sizes needed and turn them into blocks.

"I can almost see through it," marveled Gaius. "But everything on the other side of the wall is...fuzzy...unclear..."

"Yes," said Dux. "It is like the mind's eye, is it not? *Through a glass darkly.*"

Gaius wasn't sure what that meant but nodded so as not to appear stupid.

The men turned and walked along a path adjacent to the wall until they reached the East Gate. It was as enormous as the gates in the South and the West, but more elaborate. It consisted of two doors made from hazelwood planks. The planks were set in a herringbone pattern, forming endless rows of inverted Vs. Whereas the South Gate was greater in height than width, and the West Gate greater in width than height, the East

Gate formed a perfect square, with the width and height being equal.

What made the greatest impression on Gaius were the three large and complex bronze locks, arranged in the form of a triangle, that sealed the two doors of the gate shut. The locking mechanisms consisted of a bewildering array of cogged wheels, springs, pinions, weights, pistons, clutches, levers, and bolts, all of which were stamped with tiny letters, numbers, and symbols. Gaius had never seen anything so intricately contrived or mechanically complex.

CHAPTER 13

THE WARDEN OF THE EAST

Gaius was so absorbed in his analysis of the locks that he jumped at the raspy words, "Who comes here?"

He spun around to discover an elderly man standing behind him. The man wore a blue robe, like the wysards in the village, but this one was decorated with yellow stars and crescent moons. The man also wore a pointed hat, though the point had collapsed lay atop the brim. The flesh of the man's face was wrinkled and his long beard and bushy eyebrows were white, but his hazel eyes were alert.

"This," said Dux, moving forward, "is Gaius, a young man who wishes to join our Order."

The old man gave Dux a quizzical look. "What has happened to put him in such a sad state?"

Dux said, "Our travels have not been easy, Brother. We have circled the world to reach this point."

"He's already been inspected by the other Wardens, then?"

"He has."

The old man shuffled closer to Gaius. He had a slight stoop. Putting his right hand on the young traveler's shoulder, he said, "It's clear the journey has taken a toll on you. Are you sure you wish to proceed?"

"I am, sir," replied Gaius.

The Warden arched an eyebrow. "Truly?"

"Yes, sir."

"Well, you have made it this far, though you're a little worse for wear. You are not a man who is easily deterred, I think." He faced Dux. "You desire passage through the East Gate?"

"Yes."

"Your destination?"

"The Master."

The bushy eyebrows shot up. "Oh, *the Master...*"

He motioned his guests to follow him to a nearby clearing, in the center of which was a chair that seemed to be constructed of the same wood as the gate, inlaid with exquisite mother-of-pearl moons and stars. There was a bronze plate attached to the top of the chair. It contained a single word: *Dawn*. Next to the chair was a small table, and on the table was an oil lamp and an ancient book.

Sitting slowly, the Warden mumbled, "I'm not the man I used to be. I can't stand to be on my feet for too long."

Dux said, "Can you tell us where to find the Master?"

The old man smacked his lips and placed an elbow on one chair arm. Cradling his chin in his hand, he thought for a moment before saying, "I believe he was planning a trip to the center of the world."

Gaius's eyes grew large. "The center of the world? I did not know such a place existed!"

The wizard rolled his eyes. "Did you not? How could a circle or orb not have a center? Obviously, there *must* be such a place. Logic dictates." He leaned toward Gaius and tapped a finger against the young man's forehead, saying, "Think, man. Always *think*." He leaned back and said, "There is a keep there called *Heureka*. You will probably find him inside, or nearby."

"How do we get to Heureka from here?" asked Dux.

"It will not be easy, I'm afraid. There is a secret tunnel from here to there, but none know where it is other than the Master himself."

The old man thought a moment longer before saying, "However, I believe there is a fairly tolerable path that can be found somewhere in the West. You'll need to return there and ask the Warden of the West for directions. If he gives you any trouble, tell him that it was I who sent you."

Seeing the frustration on Gaius's face, he added, "To save time, you may bypass the southern realm by taking a shortcut through the caverns. Use the *Meridiem Passage*. Do you know how to find it?"

"I do," replied Dux.

"Good. Have breakfast with me. Perhaps share some tales of your travels. Then, take some time to rest. When you are ready to depart, I will unlock the East Gate for you, and you may be on your way."

CHAPTER 14

THE EASTERN WILDERNESS

The land on the opposite side of the East Gate consisted of gently rolling hills, rocky outcrops, small creeks, knee-high grass, and clusters of evergreens. Floating above the ground was a spectral mist that was illuminated by the rising sun.

"This does not seem so bad," remarked Gaius as he and his guide descended the hill on the other side of the East Gate. "Do many people live in the Eastern Wilderness?"

"Yes. Some of them are quite famous. Heraclitus, for example. There are many cities and villages here."

"Are the people here as dangerous as those in the wildernesses of the other realms?"

"Yes, I'm afraid so."

"I do not see how. I have seen how beauty and strength can be both good and bad, depending on their application, but how can wisdom ever be bad?"

"Oh, wisdom can be coupled with evil very easily. Are not some of the greatest tyrants in our world 'wise,' in a sense? They plot their evils carefully, turning their more benevolent opponents against one another. They use their understanding of human psychology and human history to gain and distribute power to their minions. It is, after all, the soul of a man, or his heart, that dictates whether wisdom is used for good or evil.

"Think also of those men who have but partial wisdom, yet imagine they have the totality. Such delusional men often close their minds to any future gains, rejecting further contemplation and the wisdom proffered by others. Anyone who challenges them, or who insinuates that there is more wisdom to be found, becomes their adversary. This, the Eastern Wilderness, is the land of such people. We know them as *zealots*, and typically they worship men and women whom they believe have the answers to all of life's questions. These objects of worship are called *gurus*, and their adherents form societies called *cults*."

"But surely no man is as wise as these zealots imagine – not even Solomon."

"You're correct, but the zealots have surrendered their minds, and so cannot be reasoned with. The members of these cults imagine that they have found 'the' answer."

"The answer to what?"

"Everything, my friend. Or, at least, everything that they believe truly matters. They are, consequently, static in mind. When one has the answer, why revisit the problem? In truth, daring to question the prescribed wisdom can be very, very dangerous."

"It is foolishness," opined Gaius with a shake of his head. "A man might be wise by the standards of his age, but he is fooling himself if the thinks that there is no greater wisdom to be found. I was taught that even the wisest man is foolish in the eyes of God."

Dux nodded. "You are the product of a virtuous education. So, you can understand why this land is dangerous. It is populated by wisdom cults and guru kings who constantly war against one another, each proclaiming that their wisdom is penultimate – that they are right in all matters and that the beliefs of all others are wrong. There is no such thing as neutrality among the zealots. There is no place for compromise, nor an open mind. For that reason, thinking men, like the members of our Order, are especially despised."

"But how shall we protect ourselves against these zealots?"

"You recall that it was Temperance that protected you in the realm of untamed beauty, and Fortitude that protected you in the realm of untamed strength, yes?"

"I do."

"What, then, do you think will protect you in the realm of foolish wisdom?"

Gaius thought for a moment. "Prudence?"

"Exactly. We must act prudentially. If confronted by a strange person or some mixed company, we must remain calm and rational. Say as little possible, and be particularly guarded if asked anything about the Order or its secrets."

No sooner had he given this advice than a group of men emerged from behind a collection of boulders some twenty yards away. Three in number, they moved toward the travelers with malign purpose, swords in hand. The one in the middle wore a battered chest plate stained with blood. All three had a peculiar metal pendant clipped to their tunics, just above their hearts.

"Stay where you are," said the man in the lead as the gang approached. He was young and well-dressed, his countenance, haughty. "Who are you, and what business have you in our fair and pure land?"

"We have no business here," replied Dux. "We are simply travelers. My name is Dux and this is my friend, Gaius. May I ask your name, sir?"

"My name is Bell," replied the gang leader, "and these are mine." He nodded toward the men alongside him, saying, "Cletus and Jones."

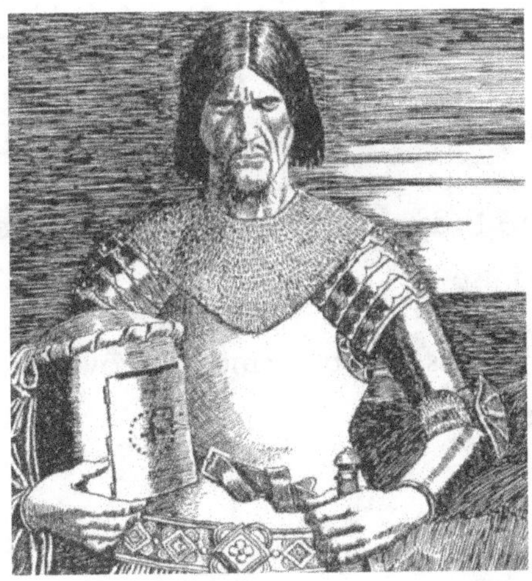

The other two men scowled. It was Cletus who wore the bloodied armor.

Bell said, "We are the guards of this path and we are charged to challenge all who use it."

Dux looked at Cletus. "Your armor is covered in fresh blood. Were you attacked?"

"No," said Bell, answering for the man. "That's not his blood. The last strangers to come down this path were pagans."

"Corrupters," mumbled Cletus.

"Troublemakers," added Jones, studying the edge of his sword. "They were dealt with in a just and appropriate manner."

"Ah," replied Dux. "Well, you'll be happy to hear that my friend and I are not troublemakers or corrupters. We are simply travelers."

Squinting, Bell replied, "Are you certain? What's that device on your walking stick?"

"An image of the sun."

"Why would you have an image of the sun on top of a stick?"

"Sun worshippers," muttered Cletus.

"No," said Dux, "we're not sun worshippers."

"What are you, then?"

"As I said, we're travelers."

"Why do you wear white armor?" asked Jones. "Only a fool would wear white armor. How do you keep it unstained?"

"By not engaging in combat unnecessarily. As you see, I have no weapon."

Cletus spat into the dirt. "Cowards, then. Deserters, maybe. Afraid to fight."

Bell tilted his head to one side and looked at Gaius. "Is that right? Are you afraid to fight? Have you lost your way and forgotten that there are things in this realm worth fighting for?"

Gaius answered, saying, "I know that there are things worth fighting for."

"Right," said Bell, nodding. "There are things worth fighting for, and things worth killing for. Or dying for." His smile was sinister. "Why don't you come back to our village and we'll teach you what's worth fighting for. We figured it out a long time ago, you see. We'll teach you all about the Principles."

"The Principles?"

Jones made a curious gesture with one hand. "The totality of all Truths," he said reverentially.

Cletus made the same gesture, then said, "But your companion has to die. There's no place for pagans here. He's already contaminated the land with his sun god and coward's armor. Unless, of course, he's willing to repent and adhere to the Principles."

Dux said, "I would love to learn about these teachings, but I'm afraid we're in a bit of a hurry. Of course, if you have a book of these teachings you'd be willing to part with-"

"Oh," said Bell, realization flashing across his face. "I know who you are! You're a member of the Order. You're as pagan as they come! There's no redemption for your kind."

He turned to Cletus and said, "Drive a nail through the old man's tongue. We'll take him back to the village, flip him upside down, and burn him alive. It's the only civilized thing to do."

"It's the only way," agreed Cletus, pulling a large iron nail from a bag attached to his belt.

"Surely not the only way," offered Dux. "Perhaps we could talk about this over some tea?"

"Tea is liquid perdition," sneered Jones. "The leaves taint the pure waters and give rise to unnatural thoughts."

"Nail the stranger's tongue down already," said Bell. "The man's ignorance has no bounds."

But Cletus had not taken his first step before a curious whizzing sound filled the air, causing him, and everyone else, to look up.

Jones said, "What was-" just before a scream of anguish escaped his lips and he fell to the ground, unconscious.

Bell rushed over to the man and bent down, touching the peculiar object that had struck Jones in the back of the head. It was shaped like a wide V and made of a hard wood that was finely polished.

He stood quickly and yelled, "Cletus!" just before an identical object struck his own forehead, sending him crumpling to the ground, also.

Cletus, nail in hand, took a step back, fear in his eyes. He was only a few feet behind the fallen bodies of his companions but seemed to have little interest in aiding them. He looked at Dux and Gaius accusingly, but seeing that they had nothing in their hands, darted his eyes further afield.

Licking his lips, he yelled, at no one in particular, "I don't want any trouble!"

"You'd best go, then," said Dux quietly. "Trouble has found you. Don't worry, I'm sure your friends will recover, albeit with aching heads."

Cletus considered this, still moving backward. "You'll kill them."

Dux lifted his chin. "And stain my white armor? I think not."

Cletus paused for a moment, seemingly considering his options. Then he gave Dux and Gaius a final withering look, turned on one heel, and ran.

When he was out of sight, Gaius said, "What good fortune is this? Who has saved us?"

Dux pointed at a man approaching them from a nearby cluster of trees. The newcomer was dressed simply in a wool tunic, britches, and boots, all brown, and he carried a leather sack in one hand. His hair was red, as was his beard. Gaius thought he was about 20 years old – very close to his own age.

The stranger extended a hand toward Dux. "Greetings, Brother. Able Cooke, at your service."

The men shook hands and Dux introduced himself and his charge, adding, "Your appearance was timely, Brother."

Gaius said, "Yes! We're very fortunate you were in the area and flew to our aid."

Able shrugged. "It wasn't fortune, exactly. I was hunting when I saw you arrive via the East gate. There's been plenty of trouble in this area lately, and as the day was young, I decided to trail you for a bit. I was careful to remain concealed, but also to remain within throwing distance. When I saw that you were in distress, I did what any brother would do."

Gaius considered this. "But how did you know we were in distress, being so far away? Could you hear what was being said? I do not mean to sound ungrateful, but from the trees in which you were hidden, which are some distance from here, it must have appeared that we were merely talking to the zealots. They had swords drawn, yes, but they had not moved to attack us. What prompted you to attack them?"

Able gave Dux a puzzled look, as if surprised at the question.

Dux said, "He's not yet a member of the Order."

"Oh," exclaimed Able, looking at Gaius. "Sorry, friend, I just assumed..." Seemingly embarrassed, he bent over and retrieved his weapons from the ground. "They didn't seem like friendly types."

"I see," said Gaius, though he did not. "What are those?"

"Ah," said Able, handing one of his missiles over. "These are called *boomerangs*. I discovered them during my travels. They're useful in hunting small game. We're lucky that the third man ran away. I only have two of these, and no other weapons. If he'd moved forward with his sword..."

"Our faith is in God," said Dux, with a wave of one hand. "I wasn't concerned. Plus, I did have this," he added, lifting his staff into the air.

Seeing Gaius's doubtful expression, he added, "A weapon of last resort, to be sure."

"Where will you go from here?" asked Abel.

"The Meridiem Passage."

"You know the way?"

"I do," answered Dux.

"Is there anything else I can do for you?"

"No, thank you. You've saved our lives, and that is enough. We're in a hurry and I'd rather not give the zealots another opportunity to attack us."

Abel nodded. "You're right to do so. The man who escaped will return with reinforcements. You'll be safer in the caverns. I'll follow you until you get there, just in case there's more trouble along the way. You may not see me, but rest assured, I will be there."

Dux shook the man's hand again. "Thank you, brother. That is a great comfort."

CHAPTER 15

THE MERIDIEM PASSAGE

Gaius and Dux traveled along the path for another hour before reaching a forest of evergreens, at which point they left the path and began following what Gaius thought was an animal trail, the trees closely spaced on either side.

"Are we still within the length of Abel's throw?" the initiate asked, worried.

"No," answered Dux, "his missiles are useless in the woods, so he has probably returned to his hunt by now. But don't fret, it is a short journey from here to the caverns."

The two walked for a period before encountering a rocky outcropping, in the center of which was the entrance to a cave, partially concealed by tall ferns.

"Here we are," said Dux, tapping his staff into the ground three times. As before, the emblem of the sun at the top began to glow. He grasped Gaius's arm. "It's dark inside, so stay close."

The interior of the cave was cool and, as promised, dark, except for the light generated by the guide's staff. Yet looking about, Gaius was surprised to discover that the interior consisted of four perfectly flat stone walls that were perpendicular to a perfectly level stone floor and ceiling. It was as if he'd stepped into the interior of a stone cube. Opposite the cave's entrance was an iron door.

"What is this place?" he asked.

"The antechamber of the Meridiem Passage," said Dux, shuffling slowly forward across the wet, slick floor. "Better known to the Order as the Ante Meridiem. Beyond this door is a staircase that will take us to an underground river named the *Timo*, which flows west. There is a dock there, too, and a boat reserved for travelers."

The iron door groaned as Dux opened it, and the men proceeded to climb down a spiral staircase on the other side. As they descended, Gaius could hear the gentle splashing of water against the cavern's walls below them. It was a soothing sound, though he knew the setting would be terrifying without the light of Dux's staff.

At the bottom of the stairs, the men stepped onto a narrow walkway consisting of rotting wooden planks bound together by wire. This walkway led them to the shore of the underground river, and, after a sharp turn, to the dock Dux had described. Attached to the dock was a four-sided post, and on each side of the post, letters had been etched from top to bottom. The letters spelled the word *Ante Meridiem*.

Gaius said, "Where is the boat?"

Dux pointed toward the darkness to his right, saying, "Be patient. It will arrive."

And it was not long before a boat *did* arrive. It was just large enough to hold two men, and on its side was painted the name, *Solaris*. It rolled gently right and left, moved by the river's current, creaking as it did so, until it bumped up against the dock, as if drawn to that specific location. There it floundered, bumping again and again into the dock's underwater supports.

Dux stepped into the boat first, placing his staff into a vertical tube built into the craft's bow. The glowing staff in place, he reached back and helped his companion aboard.

"Where are the oars?" asked Gaius, stepping forward.

"None are needed. The river's current will take us safely to the other side without our intervention."

"But wouldn't it be wise to have oars, just in case we should need to row against the current?"

"No, for no man can row against the current. Many have tried, but the current is too strong. The river will take you where it wishes to take you. There is no stopping it, or going back." Dux reached out and gently pushed the boat away from the dock, "Rest easy, now. It is midsummer, so the trip will take a little over fourteen hours."

Settling in on his bench as the boat veered right, away from the landing, Gaius said, "Why should it matter what time of year it is?"

"The path of the river changes daily. In winter, the level of water in the river is very low, and the trip from east to west is fairly straight, which means it takes less than eight hours. In summer, however, the river becomes much wider. It floods the southern bank and the stronger current takes the *Solaris* in that direction. Consequently, to go from east to west in summer, the Solaris makes a curved path that first takes us south."

"Fourteen hours is a very long time. Surely, we will be able to stop along the way?"

Dux sat as the *Solaris* began to drift away from the dock. "Yes. There are rest stops on both banks of the river called *Solstices*, and another rest stop on a small island in the middle of the river, which is called *Equinox*. All are that midpoint of our passage. We will drift to whichever is closest, and there be towed in by a man using a long pole and hook."

"Why are the rest points on the two banks called Solstices? It is a very strange name."

"It makes perfect sense if you know the source of the word, Gaius. This boat is the *Solaris*, named after the sun. So you can understand the 'Sol' part, surely."

"Yes, but what of 'stice?' I have never heard that word used."

"True, but you will know its cousins. For example, *persist, resist, assist, exist, subsist*...the list goes on and on. They all stem from the Latin word, *sistere*, which means 'to stand in one place,' or 'stop.' Thus, a Solstice is simply the point between east and west in which our boat, the *Solaris*, stops, or pauses, before continuing on its way."

"And what of this island in the river call *Equinox*?"

"It is called that because it is *equally* distant from the rest points on either bank."

With that, the conversation ended. Both men, exhausted from the day's exertions, and comforted by the coolness and darkness of the passage, drifted into a dreamless slumber.

When they awoke, many hours later, they found themselves floating very near a small, brilliantly illuminated cottage on the southern shore - the Summer Solstice. Gaius was surprised to hear the sound of laughter and music, and could see men gathered together over fires, cooking, with mugs in their hands. There were dozens of people present, and they seemed to be having a good time.

"Well, that's unfortunate," said Dux, wiping the sleep from his eyes.

"What?"

The guide turned to his friend, saying, "Each year, when the river reaches its maximum width, and the boat traffic increases to the southern shore, a great feast is held by members of our Order there. Unfortunately, you are not yet a member, which means we cannot participate."

Gaius's shoulders drooped. The food smelled wonderful. He was tired of the dry, tasteless hardtack that he and his guide had subsisted on in recent days. Wine would be wonderful, also – and music, and dancing, and jokes. Yet he knew that he was not yet worthy to partake in any of it. He let out a long breath and nodded. "I understand."

The Solaris drifted by the celebration. When the sights, sounds, and smells were behind the travelers, Gaius asked, "What is the source of the Timo – that is the name of this river, right?"

"That's right." Dux shrugged. "No one knows. Some say it has no source but flows in a continuous circle about the world, powered by a mysterious source. Some argue that the river is as old as the world. The origins and nature of the Timo are a matter of constant speculation by the wysards of the East, while the people of the South prefer to use its mystery as a source of inspiration for their poems and stories. The citizens of the West are, as ever, more industrious, and use the river to carry goods. They have also built watermills upon it, which they use to grind corn into grain."

Gaius thought for a moment, then ventured, "The Master must make this same journey often, to check in with his Wardens and survey the realms. I wonder how he has time to do anything else!"

Dux shook his head. "There's no need for the Master to personally travel to all the realms. He has officers that do that for him. Me, for example. I spend most of my time traveling at his request, and sometimes even venture into the Known World, if the Master requires it. I report everything I see. My junior counterpart, Diakonos, though primarily engaged by the Warden of the West, performs similar duties. The Master is also assisted by a treasurer, secretary, marshal, and so on."

"With all these people at his beck and call, he sounds like a king."

Dux laughed. "He is far from a king. He's more like an administrator. He suffers many of the responsibilities of a king – the ones that no man in his right mind would want - yet he enjoys none of the power. Not that he wants power. In practice, any man who desires power isn't qualified to be a Master."

Gaius said, "Is he rich?"

"Not at all. Why would you think he's rich?"

"Because he has a treasurer, and so must have a treasure."

"The *treasury* is for paying bills, Gaius. It's not for the Master's personal use."

"Doesn't he have an army? You said he had a Marshal."

"The Marshal is a figurehead who leads ceremonies from time to time. He doesn't even have a weapon; he carries a baton. Truth be told, half the time we can't find him when we need him. He's rather elusive."

Gaius thought about this, too, then said, "This is a very curious Order."

"More curious than you can imagine," replied Dux.

The two men floated from the southern bank of the river toward the southwest for several more hours, talking about various and unimportant things, until, at last, they approached a dock with a large wooden post affixed to it. Beyond the dock, there was a stone wall that extended from the ceiling to a point just above the surface of the river. The slender gap between the bottom of the wall and the river's surface would allow the Solaris to continue on its journey, but with only inches to spare.

The boat drifted toward the dock and began to bump against it, as if signaling the passengers that their portion of the journey was at an end. Dux dutifully reached out a hand and grabbed the post on the dock, pulled himself up, and retrieved his staff from the bow. He then reached out for Gaius and helped him out of the boat. Gaius saw that the post had been engraved with the following words: *Post Meridiem*.

Its burden lifted, the boat drifted away from the dock and, a moment later, disappeared beneath the narrow shelf that rested above the waters.

Dux's magical light flickered, then began to wane. The guide pointed at a nearby spiral staircase, identical to the one on the east side of the river.

He said, "We'd best hurry. I haven't got much light left to share."

CHAPTER 16

RETURN TO THE WEST

The two men emerged from the Meridiem Passage to find the sun hovering just above the western horizon. They walked for a period before the path ended at a cobblestone road that appeared to run south-north. Where the path met the road, there was an ancient wooden pole, and on it, an ancient wooden sign, on which was carved the words, "Wonthard Lane."

The forest on the west side of the cobblestone road seemed particularly dense and impenetrable.

"This doesn't seem right," said Gaius, stepping into the middle of the road and looking both ways. "This road runs only north and south. We need to go west."

Dux surveyed the road, the forest around them, and the sky above, which was now composed of pink and purple clouds. A few stars were visible.

"Ah," he said, pointing northwest at something visible just above the trees. "Do you see it?"

Gaius took a step back and looked. Because the western sky was still softly illuminated by the setting sun, he could just make out the silhouette of the object.

"The Pillar of Strength," he said, nodding. "But how shall we reach it?"

"I don't think we should attempt to cross the forest," said Dux. "That would be difficult even during the day, and we're bound to get lost in such low light. We'd lose all the time we have gained by using the Meridiem shortcut. Better that we follow this road north and hope that there is another path or road that intersects it, which will carry us further west."

The men set off, moving north, a dark, starry sky on their right and a colorful twilight sky on their left, until they did, in fact, encounter an east-west path that crossed their road. Looking west, Gaius saw that this path led directly to the Pillar of Strength, which was easily discernible due to its size.

Better, and much to his surprise, he saw the Warden of the West moving toward him, and not fifty paces away.

"Well now," yelled the Warden as he approached, "what brings you back to my realm so soon? I thought you were off to see the Master."

As he got nearer, the giant looked at Dux, the hint of a smile on his lips, and cocked an eyebrow. "Didn't get lost, I hope? I recall you have a propensity for turning right when you should turn left, and sometimes spinning in circles without purpose."

The guide frowned. "You have too good a memory, Warden. No, we're not lost. We are still in search of the Master."

"Then why are you here?"

"The Warden of the East told us that the Master is today in Heureka, at the center of the world, and that the only way to reach that place is via a secret path that originates here, in the West."

The Warden crossed his arms, his good-natured smile fading. He chewed on the inside of his cheek. "The location of that path is not to be shared with just anyone, Brother."

"I know. But it is the command of the Warden of the East that you show us the way."

The giant waited another second before dropping his hands to his hips. He nodded. "Very well."

The Warden of the West moved forward and took Gaius by his right arm. Without stopping, he pulled the young man gently forward, until the two were walking side-by-side, headed east. Dux trailed behind them.

Loudly enough for both men to hear him, the big man said, "The only way to approach Heureka from the west is through the Tessella mountains." He looked at Gaius. "You'll see the mountain range as soon as we escape the confines of the forest. It completely encircles Heureka. The mountains are very steep, each rising to a perfect, pointed peak. In the twilight, they more closely resemble massive pyramids than mountains. Some think they resemble the plated spine of a dragon. The tallest of them have snow-capped peaks."

"They must be difficult to climb if they are so steep," remarked Gaius.

"They are treacherous, yes. Many men have died in foolhardy attempts to reach Heureka by traversing them. There are very few handholds or footholds and the stone resists even the hardest climbing spikes. A single slip during an ascent means death. And while they are beautiful, they are inhospitable to life. They retain neither soil nor seed. Each time I see them, I am reminded of the many comforts I enjoy here, in the land below, where wildlife is plentiful, farms fruitful, and any man may find gainful employment."

"Why would men climb them, if they are so dangerous? Surely there are routes between the mountains that travelers could take."

The Warden shook his head. "The valleys are filled with immense piles of gravel and dust. These piles are as deep as a pond and very unstable. The gravel slides beneath your feet, filling the air with a cloud of choking dust that clogs the lungs and blinds the eyes. Worse, the gravel is razor-sharp. A single fall will slice open both your clothing and your flesh."

"Oh," said Gaius, reminded of the pain he'd endured in the North when the sands had tried to capture him. "If there is no way over the mountains, and no traversable valleys, how shall we reach Heureka?"

"Patience," replied the Warden, holding up a finger.

Gaius repressed a sigh. It seemed he might never reach the end of his journey. He wondered if he had committed some great sin and was secretly destined to travel in circles the rest of his life, his destination always being just another day away.

But, he consoled himself, was that not the fate of all men? And that being so, was it not better to be accompanied on such a journey by noble men such as the Warden and his guide, and the other fine men of the Order whom Gaius had so far encountered?

At length, the sun abandoned the trio altogether and the path through the forest was illuminated only by a crescent moon behind them. Another hour passed before the travelers emerged from the forest into a clearing where the walls of trees was replaced by a canopy of stars.

Though Gaius could not see the Tessella mountains, he was able to deduce their shape by their silhouettes against the starry background. As he'd been told, the mountains were almost perfect triangles. The reflection of the moon's light off the snow that capped the mountains gave the range a ghostly appearance.

The Warden came to a halt. "End of the road," he said. "Though the darkness hides them from your eyes, you now stand between the two ancient pillars that mark the western approach to Heureka."

Gaius looked left and right, seeing nothing but blackness. "Are they like the other great pillars - of Beauty, Strength, and Wisdom?"

"No. These pillars are far more ancient than those three. They are very different in form, material, and construction. They are not carved from stone, but rather cast in bronze. And while immense, they are hollow."

"Why are they hollow?" asked Gaius.

He heard Dux approach him, saying, "That is a discussion for another day."

Again frustrated, Gaius blew out a breath. He couldn't help but grumble, "There are ancient pillars on either side of me, yet I cannot see them. The Tessella mountains are in front of me, yet I can see only their silhouettes. I stand among some of the greatest wonders of this world, yet I am blind."

"Take heart," said the Warden. "You cannot hope to see and experience all things on your first journey. Your current objective is to meet the Master, and you are very near to doing that. One thing at a time, yes? But I offer you this consolation: You asked me how we could reach Heureka without going over the mountains, or between them. Here is your answer:

"Most of the time, the pillars on either side of us are majestic but without any special qualities. At other times, however, under very specific circumstances, and for a very short period, a portal is formed between them. Anyone who steps into the portal is instantly transported to Heureka. I am happy to report that such circumstances exist at this very moment."

"A portal," said Gaius, chewing on the word. "A doorway, you mean?"

"No. Something more magical."

"More magical than non-magical," offered Dux.

"It will take you from here to Heureka in but a few steps," said the Warden. "However, because you are not a member of our Order yet, it would be unwise for you to enter it alone and unannounced. I'll go first. Once I am on the other side, I will extend my hand. Take it, and I will pull you through. Do you understand?"

"Yes," said Gaius, but he was afraid.

Apparently sensing the young man's fear, the Warden said, "Don't worry. There's nothing on the other side that can harm you, and Dux will be right behind you."

Gaius cleared his throat. "I'm not afraid."

"Glad to hear it. Alright, then. Here we go…" And with that, the hazy silhouette of the Warden vanished. Then came the words, "Give me your hand."

It was the Warden's voice, but it sounded oddly distant. Nor was there any visual hint that the man had returned.

Gaius slowly lifted his right arm and reached into the darkness. He felt the Warden's large hand seize his own and pull him forward. As he advanced, Gaius felt the hairs on his arm stand up, as if the portal carried an electrical charge. The air seemed suddenly thinner, warmer, and more humid. The smell of the forest vanished, replaced by a scent he was unfamiliar with, which was neither pleasing nor displeasing.

The darkness persisted. As his leading foot touched the ground on the other side of the portal, Gaius felt suddenly dizzy. He swayed, but the Warden steadied him.

"Easy does it," said the other man, holding Gaius upright. "Don't panic. Just bring your other foot forward slowly…there you go. The sense of vertigo will pass. Just stand still and breathe normally."

Gaius struggled to stand erect. He felt sick. But as the Warden had promised, within seconds, the vertigo evaporated, as did the nausea.

The Warden released the traveler, allowing him to stand on his own.

He said, "I've got to return to the West now, Gaius. That gate isn't going to guard itself and there's probably already a line of workers waiting to be paid. It's been a pleasure meeting you. Come see me again, eh?"

Before Gaius could formulate a response, the Warden was gone.

CHAPTER 17

DISCOVERING THE MASTER

A violent wind blew in from the East.

It came so suddenly that it nearly knocked Gaius off his feet. It was followed by another of even greater strength.

Troubled, Gaius said, "Are you there, Dux?"

"I am," replied the guide, confirming that he, too, had stepped through the portal.

"Where do we go from here?"

"Nowhere," answered the guide. "The Master must come to us, now."

Uneasy with the darkness and the wind, Gaius said, "Perhaps you can use your staff to make light, as you did before."

"I'm sorry, but the staff's magic is exhausted."

"Then shouldn't we at least seek shelter? I think there is a storm coming. The wind howls around us, and behind it, I hear a strange sound, like the roar of lions."

"What you hear is the crashing of waves against the shore. We stand on a small, rocky island in the midst of a tumultuous sea."

Gaius frowned. This was very unwelcome news. A sea? How was that possible? The last place Gaius wanted to be was stranded on a rocky outcrop in the middle of a violent sea, in blackness.

He said, "I thought the portal would take us to a point within the mountains."

"It has, but time and space have a curious relationship here, and we have traveled through both. This is the right place, as it was long ago. This is the world primeval, crude, and primitive. There is no other life here. No sentience. No purpose. It is, you might say, *tabula rasa*. A blank slate."

"You are saying that we have traveled back in time, to the beginning of our world?"

"Yes, and if you think on it, you will comprehend that this beginning is symbolic of many beginnings. That is why the Master is here. This is where your journey as a member of our Order truly begins."

"Do you mean that the Master *planned* to meet me here?"

Before Dux could answer, a voice emerged from the darkness directly ahead.

"No, Gaius. I *hoped* to meet you here. Not all men make it this far."

Startled, Gaius replied, "Sir, I cannot see you, but your voice is familiar. Do I know you?"

The unseen man replied, "Yes. You know me as a friend, and I hope you will soon know me as a brother. But let me advise you to think hard about what you are about to do. Though you have survived several trials at the gates, there are more perils to be endured if you join us. There are privileges, yes, and joys, but with those benefits come toil, obligations, and dangers."

Gaius did not hesitate. "Then I will endure them."

"But you do not know their nature, my friend. What if the obligations are wicked, the dangers pointless, and the toil excessive?"

Gaius considered this. "I am not concerned about toil or dangers," he said. "But I would ask your assurance that there is no wickedness or evil in the obligations. If I must commit to doing anything immoral, then I will abandon my quest."

"Well said. In that case, you have my assurance, and my word, that, indeed, the obligations are noble and good. Like you, all members of our Order are men of faith who love their families and communities, and obey the almighty God. We are a just society, rendering unto every man what he due, without distinction. You will be treated justly, and we require that you treat others in the same manner, whether or not they are members of our Order."

These words warmed Gaius's heart. "Then I wish to proceed, sir."

The final word had barely escaped Gaius's lip when there was a frightening flash of lightning behind the dark clouds above him, followed by a deafening boom. Gaius instinctively cringed, covering his eyes to guard them against the light.

When he recovered, he saw that the land around him was not quite as dark as it had been only seconds before. The previously impenetrable clouds had thinned, allowing the sun and moon to dart a few rays of light into the world below them.

Then, a third light appeared, this one directly in front of Gaius. It was, the traveler saw, the light of a newly lit taper, or thin candle, just a few paces away. Though a thick fog concealed the carrier's identity, Gaius assumed the taper was held by the Master.

"May I ask who you are, sir?" he said.

"You will discover that soon enough, my friend. But first, tell me why you are here. What is it that you are in search of? I caution you to think before you answer."

Gaius did think, and did answer, and the answer was correct.

And here the story ends, for what follows no man can know, lest he is himself a traveler. Yet it can be revealed that, once Gaius was sworn into the Order, and gifted the immaculate white armor envied by even kings and potentates, he embarked upon still greater adventures, seeking, with his brethren, that which was lost

AUTHOR'S CLOSING REMARKS

I hope you enjoyed this tale of allusions. Some closing comments:

The illustrations in this story are from 19th-century books now in the public domain. I sorted through hundreds of illustrations to find ones that were appropriate to the scenes being depicted.

However, my initial plan was to include *original* artwork. Toward that end, I hired two separate artists, but I was so dissatisfied with what they submitted that I elected not to use their work. If this book is well received, I'll probably redouble my efforts to find an artist or illustrator who can provide original material. I am always open to suggestions, so feel free to contact me if you have a recommendation. If you are both a brother and an artist, so much the better.

I am also open to suggestions on how I might improve upon this story. Are there important elements that I've missed that could be easily included? Let me know. Again, I have no illusions that this Masonic tale will be read by anyone other than members of our fraternity, and its purpose is purely educational, so I am not averse to recommendations regarding how it might be improved. Please send any comments, corrections, or recommendations to:

Bob Lingerfelt

1927LA@gmail.com

Thank you!

ALSO BY BOB W. LINGERFELT

Solomon's Memory Palace